Obvious? Isn't It Obvious? Is
Obvious? Isn't It Obvious? Is
Obvious? Isn't It Obvious? Is
Obvious? Isn't It Obvious? Is
Obvious? Isn't It Obvious? Isn't It Obvious? Isn't It Obvious? Is
Obvious? Isn't It Obvious? Isn't It Obvious? Isn't It Obvious? Is
Obvious? Isn't It Obvious? Isn't It Obvious? Isn't It Obvious? Is
Obvious? Isn't It Obvious? Isn't It Obvious? Isn't It Obvious? Is
Obvious? Isn't It Obvious? Isn't It Obvious? Isn't It Obvious? Is
Obvious? Isn't It Obvious? Isn't It Obvious? Isn't It Obvious? Is
Obvious? Isn't It Obvious? Isn't It Obvious? Isn't It Obvious? Is
Obvious? Isn't It Obvious? Isn't It Obvious? Isn't It Obvious? Is
Obvious? Isn't It Obvious? Isn't It Obvious? Isn't It Obvious? Is
Obvious? Isn't It Obvious? Isn't It Obvious? Isn't It Obvious? Is
Obvious? Isn't It Obvious? Isn't It Obvious? Isn't It Obvious? Is
Obvious? Isn't It Obvious? Isn't It Obvious? Isn't It Obvious? Is
Obvious? Isn't It Obvious? Isn't It Obvious? Isn't It Obvious? Is
Obvious? Isn't It Obvious? Isn't It Obvious? Isn't It Obvious? Is
Obvious? Isn't It Obvious? Isn't It Obvious? Isn't It Obvious? Is
Obvious? Isn't It Obvious? Isn't It Obvious? Isn't It Obvious? Is
Obvious? Isn't It Obvious? Isn't It Obvious? Isn't It Obvious? Is
Obvious? Isn't It Obvious? Isn't It Obvious? Isn't It Obvious? Is
Obvious? Isn't It Obvious? Isn't It Obvious? Isn't It Obvious? Is
Obvious? Isn't It Obvious? Isn't It Obvious? Isn't It Obvious? Is
Obvious? Isn't It Obvious? Isn't It Obvious? Isn't It Obvious? Is
Obvious? Isn't It Obvious? Isn't It Obvious? Isn't It Obvious? Is
Obvious? Isn't It Obvious? Isn't It Obvious? Isn't It Obvious? Is
Obvious? Isn't It Obvious? Isn't It Obvious? Isn't It Obvious? Is
Obvious? Isn't It Obvious? Isn't It Obvious? Isn't It Obvious? Is
Obvious? Isn't It Obvious? Isn't It Obvious? Isn't It Obvious? Is
Obvious? Isn't It Obvious? Isn't It Obvious? Isn't It Obvious? Is
Obvious? Isn't It Obvious? Isn't It Obvious? Isn't It Obvious? Is
Obvious? Isn't It Obvious? Isn't It Obvious? Isn't It Obvious? Is
Obvious? Isn't It Obvious? Isn't It Obvious? Isn't It Obvious? Is
Obvious? Isn't It Obvious? Isn't It Obvious? Isn't It Obvious? Is
Obvious? Isn't It Obvious? Isn't It Obvious? Isn't It Obvious? Is
Obvious? Isn't It Obvious? Isn't It Obvious? Isn't It Obvious? Is
Obvious? Isn't It Obvious? Isn't It Obvious? Isn't It Obvious? Is

n't It Obvious? Isn't It Obvious? Isn't It Obvious? Isn't It Obvious
n't It Obvious? Isn't It Obvious? Isn't It Obvious? Isn't It Obvious
n't It Obvious? Isn't It Obvious? Isn't It Obvious? Isn't It Obvious
n't It Obvious? Isn't It Obvious? Isn't It Obvious? Isn't It Obvious
n't It Obvious? Isn't It Obvious? Isn't It Obvious? Isn't It Obvious
n't It Obvious? Isn't It Obvious? Isn't It Obvious? Isn't It Obvious
n't It Obvious? Isn't It Obvious? Isn't It Obvious? Isn't It Obvious
n't It Obvious? Isn't It Obvious? Isn't It Obvious? Isn't It Obvious
n't It Obvious? Isn't It Obvious? Isn't It Obvious? Isn't It Obvious
n't It Obvious? Isn't It Obvious? Isn't It Obvious? Isn't It Obvious
n't It Obvious? Isn't It Obvious? Isn't It Obvious? Isn't It Obvious
n't It Obvious? Isn't It Obvious? Isn't It Obvious? Isn't It Obvious
n't It Obvious? Isn't It Obvious? Isn't It Obvious? Isn't It Obvious
n't It Obvious? Isn't It Obvious? Isn't It Obvious? Isn't It Obvious
n't It Obvious? Isn't It Obvious? Isn't It Obvious? Isn't It Obvious
n't It Obvious? Isn't It Obvious? Isn't It Obvious? Isn't It Obvious
n't It Obvious? Isn't It Obvious? Isn't It Obvious? Isn't It Obvious
n't It Obvious? Isn't It Obvious? Isn't It Obvious? Isn't It Obvious
n't It Obvious? Isn't It Obvious? Isn't It Obvious? Isn't It Obvious
n't It Obvious? Isn't It Obvious? Isn't It Obvious? Isn't It Obvious
n't It Obvious? Isn't It Obvious? Isn't It Obvious? Isn't It Obvious
n't It Obvious? Isn't It Obvious? Isn't It Obvious? Isn't It Obvious
n't It Obvious? Isn't It Obvious? Isn't It Obvious? Isn't It Obvious
n't It Obvious? Isn't It Obvious? Isn't It Obvious? Isn't It Obvious
n't It Obvious? Isn't It Obvious? Isn't It Obvious? Isn't It Obvious
n't It Obvious? Isn't It Obvious? Isn't It Obvious? Isn't It Obvious
n't It Obvious? Isn't It Obvious? Isn't It Obvious? Isn't It Obvious
n't It Obvious? Isn't It Obvious? Isn't It Obvious? Isn't It Obvious
n't It Obvious? Isn't It Obvious? Isn't It Obvious? Isn't It Obvious
n't It Obvious? Isn't It Obvious? Isn't It Obvious? Isn't It Obvious
n't It Obvious? Isn't It Obvious? Isn't It Obvious? Isn't It Obvious
n't It Obvious? Isn't It Obvious? Isn't It Obvious? Isn't It Obvious
n't It Obvious? Isn't It Obvious? Isn't It Obvious? Isn't It Obvious
n't It Obvious? Isn't It Obvious? Isn't It Obvious? Isn't It Obvious
n't It Obvious? Isn't It Obvious? Isn't It Obvious? Isn't It Obvious
n't It Obvious? Isn't It Obvious? Isn't It Obvious? Isn't It Obvious
n't It Obvious? Isn't It Obvious? Isn't It Obvious? Isn't It Obvious
n't It Obvious? Isn't It Obvious? Isn't It Obvious? Isn't It Obvious

Isn't It Obvious

Isn't It Obvious

By

Eliyahu M. Goldratt

With Ilan Eshkoli and Joe Leer Brown

Productivity & Quality Publishing Pvt. Ltd.

Madras

Isn't It Obvious
ISBN: 9788185984339

This Indian edition of **Isn't It Obvious** is published by arrangement with the author for sale only in India, Pakistan, Nepal, Bangladesh, Bhutan, Sri Lanka and Maldives

Published by:

Productivity & Quality Publishing Pvt. Ltd.
38, Thanikachalam Road,
T. Nagar, Madras 600017
India
Phone : +01-(044)-2434 4519
Fax : +01-(044)-2434 2009
Email : service@kkbooks.com
www.pqp.in
www.goldratt.gen.in

Printed by:

Sudarsan Graphics Private Limited
27, Neelakanta mehta street
T. Nagar, Madras 600017.
India

Contents

Contents

Chapter 1

"Fifty percent off!"

Staring at the big red sign, Paul White wondered where his dreams had gone wrong. *I really don't have the strength for another one of these days*, he thought, and took another sip from his cup of freshly ground coffee. A long, deep breath later, Paul straightened his standard blue blazer and stepped inside the Boca Raton branch of Hannah's Shop.

Little red signs promoting the discounts, offspring of the bigger one outside, decorated the store. As the store manager, he had attached a lot of hope to this sale's success. However, the lines at the checkout counters were no longer than usual, and the products on sale were still piled high. The lower prices were not enough of an incentive. As he ran a hand through his graying hair, Paul shrugged.

Was there anything else that could be done?

It wasn't news that this store was not a huge success, but this morning Paul had received the monthly report. The Boca store had dropped down to eighth place in profitability out of the ten stores in the region. It was a new low for him.

Trying to shake off the uncomfortable feeling, he walked through the 35,000 square feet comprising the store's six departments, all of which were his responsibility. He passed the carefully laid out sheets and duvets on display in splashes of blue and green. Paul stopped for a moment to survey the mock bathroom they had set up, where thick, body-length towels hung next to bathrobes. Across from him were the kitchen textiles, where aprons and towels mingled, next to tables set with matching tablecloths, cloth napkins, and placemats in autumn shades. The carpet and rug department presented colors and textures from around the world, and then came the flowing curtains, in shades of white, gold, and silver.

The store always had a wide variety of goods, and he had worked hard to have a beautiful display maintained at all times. Trying to be constantly responsive to his customers, Paul had initiated a work plan of changing the in-store display twice as often as the front windows. The store offered attractive prices and promotions, but sales were still not taking off. Was there anything else that could be done?

A young staff trainee passed by and said hello. Paul returned the greeting with a full smile, while inwardly he reasoned that if he couldn't create more sales, perhaps staff should be dismissed. It was not something he wanted to do, but cutting one member of the sales staff meant saving some twenty thousand dollars a year. As he looked around, he saw that even though they were not in the middle of a holiday rush, all his salespeople were busy. There was no way he could let any of them go without placing some sales at risk. The store was running at reasonable manpower costs.

So, what else could be done?

"Excuse me, miss," Paul overheard an elderly lady with bronze glasses saying to Janine, one of his department managers. Pointing to a maroon tablecloth she asked, "Do you have this in sixty inches?"

"I'm afraid not," Janine replied. "We have two ninety-inch cloths left in this color, and the sixty-inch only in blue and beige. Would you prefer it in another color? Maybe one with a different pattern?"

"No, thanks. It's for my sister, and maroon is her favorite color."

As the elderly woman turned away, disappointed, Paul approached her. "Excuse me, ma'am," he offered, trying not to loom over her despite his six-foot-three frame. "Perhaps I can be of assistance. Would you like me to check if I can obtain the tablecloth from one of the chain's nearby stores?"

She agreed, and a call was placed to the Boynton Beach store. "Gary, do you have any of the maroon tablecloths, serial KTL 1860? That's the sixty-inch ones."

"Lemme check," Gary said in a nasal voice, and Paul could hear him speaking with his staff on the other side of the line. "Yes, we do, but only one."

"I have a customer who would like to buy it. Any chance you could send it over?"

"Sorry, Paul, no can do."

"I guess this is what you call teamwork," Paul said bitterly, rolling his eyes.

"If you really want to talk teamwork, instead of me sending you the tablecloth, how about sending the customer here? It will be a lot less of a hassle for everyone."

Disappointed with his colleague, Paul decided to try another tack. He called Roger, the regional warehouse manager. Their daughters were in school together, and the families had become friends. "Hi, Rog. Sorry to bother you, but I've got a request. Any chance you can get me a serial KTL 1860 tablecloth?"

"Sure, Paul. I can add it to your next shipment, on Wednesday."

"Thanks, Roger, let me double check with the customer and I'll call you back."

Paul hung up and turned to the elderly lady. "Ma'am, I'm happy to inform you that the tablecloth can be here on Wednesday," he reported, with the best customer service smile he could muster.

"Oh, I'm not sure," she said coolly. "I'm busy on Wednesdays, and I don't want to leave it for the last minute. Maybe, if I find the time, I'll stop in."

Paul watched in dismay as she left the store, and cursed under his breath the fact that he had bothered to intervene. He had just intensified his catch-22. It was almost certain this woman would not come back for the tablecloth. That meant that the tablecloth would end up as surplus for the store. He was already running a sale to get rid of his surplus stock, at little or no profit. There was no need to fill the store with items that wouldn't move fast enough. But if he didn't order it and she came in, she would be so disappointed that he would not only lose a sale but he would lose a customer. Risk losing sales or risk surpluses? This dilemma was drowning him. No wonder his store's profits weren't higher. If only he knew exactly what the customers would buy...

He called Roger again. "Send me the tablecloth, please, Rog. I'll fill the special order form when I get back to my desk. I just hope someone will buy it." And then Paul added, "Roger, do you have a crystal ball in stock?"

"I've asked the head office for two, but they said it'll take a while." Roger's smile was almost audible.

As Paul hung up, he asked himself again if there was something else that could be done to boost his store's profitability. And the answer was a simple no. Sales versus surplus was a dilemma that only a crystal ball could solve.

Chapter 2

Caroline stepped onto the porch of her parents' waterfront house, carrying her father's cell phone. Closing the glass doors behind her, she caught a reflection of her children playing catch on the large lawn, between the house and the bay. The palm trees that stood vigil around the porch her parents had recently renovated cast a pleasant shadow in the late afternoon.

Striding toward her father and his second in command, Christopher, Caroline passed behind her husband, Paul, who was deep in conversation with her mother and Christopher's wife, Jackie.

"I thought the Muniz piece was extremely powerful," Lydia, Caroline's mother, said. "A wonderful tribute."

"It was arranged so well." Jackie turned to Caroline and asked, "Dear, did you get to the opening of the Miami Art Museum anniversary exhibit?"

"No, I was abroad at the time,": she replied.

"I took Lisa and Ben to the show," Paul said, smiling

Pecking him on the cheek, Caroline added, "I think the kids enjoyed it," and then she walked toward the grill.

"Dad, you're as forgetful as Ben," Caroline said, and handed Henry Aaronson his cell phone. There were many resemblances between the two. The daughter had inherited his black hair and sharp brown eyes, as well as his stubborn determination. The stocky, charismatic man looked surprised at having forgotten the phone.

"Did it miss me terribly?" he joked. Henry took a break from turning the burgers on the grill and quickly checked if he had missed anything important. Seeing that there had been neither new calls nor new text messages, he slipped the phone into his pocket. Pointing at his grandchildren playing catch he added, "If Ben inherited my memory, I hope he also got my pitching abilities. Christopher, remember that game against Miami Senior High?"

Christopher stood a full head over his best friend and boss. "Yes, I remember your one no-hitter. I also remember that earlier we were discussing some changes Caroline wanted to make in the new computer system. I really think we have to stop introducing new changes."

"I know that my department needs this feature. It's not a question of maybe," she argued ardently. Caroline was head of purchasing for the Hannah's Shop chain, and she strove for perfection in all aspects of acquisitions. "It will allow us to manage bids and pricing much more efficiently."

"My dear," Christopher replied. "We can't keep making changes. The endless so-called improvements have been causing dysfunction for over a year now. Enough is enough. In a short while, you'll be calling the shots. For now, I need you to accept that these changes could well mean a disaster."

"I think we can consider her recommendation, if it will save us money in the long run," Henry intervened. "Get me an evaluation from the computer division by Tuesday."

Seeing that Paul had joined the kids, who were tossing a ball around, it struck Caroline that she was again wasting precious quality time on work. The kids were growing up so fast, and before she knew it, this kind of fun would become a fleeting memory.

"Yes, Dad, I'll get the evaluation ASAP," she said, and grabbing a glove from the corner of the porch, bounced over to stand between Ben and Lisa. "Count me in!" she called.

* * *

As dessert was served, Henry stood up. He looked at the small group of family and friends who had assembled in honor of Lydia's birthday. Caroline, Paul, and their kids; Henry's right-hand man, Christopher and his wife, Jackie; Gloria, Lydia's childhood friend, and her current husband.

"Some forty years ago I fell in love with the most beautiful girl who ever entered my mother's store," Henry related while holding his wife's hand tenderly. "I knew immediately I wanted to spend the rest of my life with you. As you have said so many times, and justifiably so, I have spent too much time at work. It is time I made my wish come true. This year will be my last as president of Hannah's Shop."

"Henry dear, you'll never leave it—you love the company too much," Lydia chided. "It's your baby."

"So I'll leave it to my other baby," he answered.

"Caroline will run the show perfectly without me."

Paul froze in his seat, and Caroline started to protest, "Dad, this is neither the time—"

"UNCLE DARREN!" thirteen-year-old Ben yelled at the handsome, black-haired man who stood quietly smiling in the veranda doorway.

"Surprise!" Darren exclaimed, and he walked over and hugged Lydia. "Happy birthday, Mom! I would have come earlier, but there was a delay at La Guardia."

"There would be no delay if you worked in Miami," Henry scolded. "And then we could see the twins more and not only on holidays."

"Nice to see you, too, Dad." Caroline's older brother sat down between his niece and nephew, giving each a hug. "But didn't you just say you're going to have a lot of time, to maybe visit your grandkids, real soon?"

"Would you like something to eat?" Lydia cut in, providing, as always, a buffer between her husband and son. "We can cook up a burger for you in no time."

"No thanks, Ma. I'll just take double portions of dessert."

Caroline leaned over and kissed her brother on the cheek. As Paul passed his old roommate some cake, he said, "We have a lot to talk about."

Chapter 3

"I could have taken a car service, you know," Darren said as he buckled up.

Paul had insisted on driving his old college roommate to the airport. "It's been so long since we had a quiet talk, just the two of us. I thought I should grab the opportunity," Paul answered, waiting for a traffic light to change. "So … you seeing anybody special these days?"

"Are you channeling my mother? No, not right now. Work takes up too much of my time."

"Some big project keeping you up at night?" Paul asked as he pulled the Grand Cherokee onto the Broad Causeway. Traffic was not very heavy.

"I'm involved in a number of initiatives, and any one of them could turn into something big overnight," Darren replied, and his gray-blue eyes sparkled. "The world of venture capital is full of surprises. Actually, I think I closed a last-minute deal a mere fifteen minutes before showing up yesterday."

"And I thought you came to Florida for your mother's birthday," Paul said. "Anyway, I was sure that by now you wouldn't have to work so hard on every deal. Shouldn't opportunities be chasing you, not vice versa?"

"Yeah, I thought so too," Darren said, tapping his long fingers on the window and staring out at the water. "But until I find my own niche, this is how it works. You need to have a reputation as a maven in order for opportunities to be chasing you."

"I see. So, until then you kill yourself so someone else can have long-term profits, while all you're left with is the finder's fee. Wouldn't you rather be the big boss, instead of just the middleman?"

"Hold on, I see where this is going." Darren shifted in his seat to look straight at his brother-in-law. "Are you talking about investments or about home textiles?"

"I think you should consider coming back to the company," Paul said determinedly. Turning onto I-95, he added, "We all know it's you Henry has always wanted as his successor."

"There is no way I am going to come back to run my father's company. I moved to New York to make something for myself," Darren asserted. "What's more, as far as I can see, home textiles is a slow industry; nothing really changes. In ventures, the sky's the limit. There are always new directions for development, always something exciting just around the corner."

"Yeah, maybe you're right." Even if it was a long shot, Paul reasoned, he had to check if Darren's determination had softened. Apparently it hadn't.

"Of course I'm right," was the response. "Besides, Caroline will be a good president."

"She'll make a great president, but when that happens, I won't be able to leave the firm."

"Leave?" Darren was genuinely surprised. "What are you talking about?"

"Darren, you know I'm stuck with this store."

"You've been stuck before, and every time you managed to unstick yourself and astonish everybody. You were desperate when you were in the acquisition department and then you came up with that brilliant criteria set for opening new stores. A lot of it has been incorporated into the company's expansion plan. I know you better than you think, Mr. White." The handsome venture capitalist had never seen his best friend at such a low. Trying to raise Paul's spirits, Darren continued, "Remember in college, when you fell behind in the last year because you used any excuse to run down to Florida to see Cara? Nevertheless, you placed third in our year. I'm confident you will find your way out of this rut."

"I wish I shared your confidence," Paul shrugged. "Since I took over in Boca, the store has only declined in the rankings; this quarter it dropped to eighth place."

"So maybe you shouldn't be running a store. You've got a different kind of smarts, the smarts needed to manage big systems. Come your next promotion, you'll find your bearings again, hit a strong point."

"Remember the condition I made when I joined the company?" Paul asked, rhetorically.

"No shortcuts. You wanted to start at the bottom. To move from one position to another, so that you could learn every aspect of the company."

"Yes, but no shortcuts means that I insist on not being promoted unless I deserve the promotion. The most important lesson I learned from my dad was that getting medals that you didn't earn, didn't really earn, is the most damaging thing to yourself, to your self-esteem, to your integrity."

More of Coach White's wise words, Darren thought. *They're almost as bad as the rules my father spouts whenever he can.*

Paul continued, "It was my idea to start from the trenches and work my way up, instead of being parachuted to an executive position, married to the president's daughter. Darren, you don't want to feel like the son of, so why are you surprised that I will never agree to be just the son-in-law?"

"I don't see the problem. You've moved around a lot in the company, and have a lot of experience. You've proven your worth every step of the way. What else do you want?"

"Almost every step," Paul countered. "In every other position I made a change. Not always the biggest change, but somehow I left an imprint of some kind. But here, in the heart of Hannah's Shop's business, in managing a store, I failed. Maybe it's because I've got the worst location possible, in that old, ugly mall. Maybe it's because my clientele is all rich, older ladies, and the chain is geared towards the middle class. All these excuses don't change the fact that I haven't proven my value in this most crucial step."

"Maybe you just need a little more time?"

"That's my problem. I don't have much time left." Paul seemed upset. "I've been there for three years. A year ago, the pressure to move me up started, so I stalled as much as I could, trying to buy time. But judging by my performance, there are so many other people who deserve to be promoted before me. Darren, if you know me, you know too well that I will never accept it. No way."

Paul avoided a speeding motorcycle and continued, "In any case, the promotion is looming just around the corner. In six months I should be learning the ropes in my next position. Until last night, it was clear to me that I had half a year to either improve things or leave, and then Henry goes and ruins that option as well."

"Why? Because he's handing the reins over to Cara?" The question was inevitable. "For years we've known—everybody knew that it was in the pipeline. And why should that stop you from leaving? Cara will understand the complexity of your situation, and won't take it personally." *And maybe if Paul leaves*, he thought, *it will show the old man that this firm is not the heaven on earth he thinks it is, that not everyone fits in there.*

"As long as the promotion was just in the pipeline, I had time." Paul explained, "Frankly, Henry's always talked about retirement but until yesterday he never gave a specific date. We all assumed it wouldn't happen for many years. And by then the kids would be older."

"The kids? You mean your kids? What do they have to do with it?"

"Currently," Paul answered, "with the constant business turbulences, Cara is often overseas, so I'm at home with Ben and Lisa. With the presidency, she'll have even less time for them. You know very well that I won't be able to find an appropriate job that doesn't require a lot of travel. With a promotion inside the company, I could have managed. Cara and I would have coordinated our trips not to coincide. But I won't be able to do that if I work outside Hannah's Shop. That means that the kids won't have either of us during those crucial years. Lisa's only nine!"

"And you won't argue that your self-fulfillment is more important than Cara's, or than your kids' needs," Darren concluded, truly understanding his friend. "And instead of asking her to give up her dream job, you're asking me to come and steal it from her?"

"But it's not her dream job."

"Are you kidding me? Hannah's Shop is her life." Darren gave Paul a funny look. "Did she say she doesn't want the job?"

"Not in those words," Paul replied. "The thing is, Caroline has always said that purchasing fits her like a glove. Predicting market trends, choosing the new collections, squeezing the best deals from the suppliers:

that's what she's so good at, that's what she loves. She will hate being president, the top administrator, immersed in numbers and petty, ego-driven politics. I know she'll be miserable."

"So you want me to ride in on my white steed, wave my sword around, take the presidency by storm, rescue the fair maiden, and save the day for all?" Darren could not help but smile. "Dude, I love you to death, but you're asking a bit much here."

"I know, I know," Paul apologized. "But it was worth a shot."

"You'll have to tough it out, I guess."

"Yeah."

"And what does Caroline say about you contemplating leaving?"

"She doesn't know yet." Paul slowed down, allowing a gray van to overtake them. "I couldn't find a way to tell her. For years she has said how great it will be when we can drive to work together. I don't know how to tell her that it won't be happening."

"You have to," Darren said as they pulled into Miami International Airport. "If there's one thing I've learned from my divorce, it's that you should discuss what troubles you, as early as possible."

Pulling up outside the departures terminal, Paul answered, "I know. I just have to figure out how." When the right moment came, Paul rationalized, he would tell Cara. Before then, hopefully a solution would come his way, making that burdensome conversation completely unnecessary.

"And if you end up leaving the firm," Darren said as he opened the car door to let himself out, "give me a call. You know I appreciate your talents."

Chapter 4

Paul was brushing his teeth when his cell phone rang. Caroline reached across the king-size bed to his nightstand and answered it.

"Oh, I see," she said, getting up and walking to the bathroom. "Honey, it's the alarm company."

Quickly rinsing his mouth, he took the phone.

"Yes?"

"Mr. White, this is Darla from Granbury Emergency Services. A water leak has been detected in the A-5 warehouse facilities at the Boca Beach Mall." Her voice was almost metallic. Paul ended the call and went back to brushing his teeth. One of the most aggravating aspects of having a cell phone was that people who monitored the alarms that went off by themselves could find you anywhere, anytime.

As he pulled on a pair of gray slacks, the cell phone rang again.

"Good morning, Ted," Paul greeted his floor manager brightly. "Everything ready at the store for the new collection to arrive?"

"Yes, but we have a big problem. A huge problem." Paul's smile faded at Ted's reply. "A pipe burst in the storeroom ceiling. There's water everywhere. They just closed the main pipes, so I will be able to go in and see in a minute."

"How much water are we talking about?" Paul asked, and sat down to put on his socks and shoes.

"I have no idea—a lot. I don't know what the damages are yet, but I heard John from Kaffee Books saying that all their stock was destroyed."

"I'm on my way."

Paul told Caroline about the situation, asked her to apologize to the kids for missing breakfast, and ran out the door, jacket and tie in hand.

Driving toward I-95, Paul called his floor manager.

"Ted, give me a short report."

"It looks like most of the boxes weren't touched," Ted informed him, and Paul sighed in relief. "We're taking all the boxes that were damaged upstairs."

"Once those are all upstairs, have some of the staff go through the boxes to see what can be salvaged, but keep bringing up the rest of the boxes," Paul demanded. "The dampness and the smells could easily get into the textiles."

"Should I put them in the parking lot?"

Paul made a quick decision as he turned onto the interstate. "No, put it all inside the store. Call me in half an hour with an update."

His jeep had never been driven so fast before.

On the sixth try, somewhere near Aventura, Paul finally got through to the mall manager. "Raul, it's Paul from Hannah's Shop. I'm on my way to the mall. How bad is it?"

"Paul, I can't talk right now. Don't worry, everything's under control. Our contractor is already here, and within three or four days, I'm sure everything will be back to normal." Raul hung up before Paul could ask any more questions.

As Paul approached Deerfield Beach, Ted called.

"Yes, Ted."

"We cleared out all the boxes that got damaged and are checking the goods," he said. "Mike and Isabella just got here, so we started to bring up the rest of the boxes, as you requested."

"Thanks, Ted. I'll be there in about ten minutes."

Paul was grateful his most responsible subordinate had arrived early that morning. It is always good to know you have someone you can rely on.

Pulling into his reserved parking space, Paul could not help staring at the piles of wet books and shoe boxes in the parking lot. Damn, he thought, that's a lot of damage. Kadence, the owner of Kaffee Books, was standing dumb-founded on her loading dock. The sight was startling, and Paul began to fear that Ted had underestimated the real damage to his store's goods.

Paul entered his store through the loading dock. He nodded to one of the floor staff who was waiting with an empty hand truck next to the service elevator. Quickly moving past his office, the Boca store manager had to see how the store had fared. Inside, beneath hearts and arrows celebrating Valentine's Day, a human chain had been set up, and his staff was working hard bringing in the merchandise. He approached Ted, who was standing next to three salespeople unpacking and checking goods.

"What's the damage?"

"We were lucky, boss," the younger man replied. "I think the plastic wrapping protected most of the merchandise in the waterlogged cartons. But we lost a few rolls of wall-to-wall carpet and a number of drapes, we're not sure yet how many."

Paul was relieved. Considering his neighbor's situation, he had really been fortunate. "Thank you, Ted. You're doing a great job," Paul said honestly. He turned to all his employees and said, "You're all doing great. I really appreciate your efforts and the teamwork. Thank you so much."

Looking at the situation, it was clear to Paul that the store would not open that day. In order to be able to open tomorrow, he had to clear the stock as soon as possible. "I'm going to the storeroom," he told the sandy-haired man from south Miami. "I need to see it with my own eyes."

The first thing that hit Paul as he stepped out of the service elevator was the smell of damp. A lot of water must have damaged a lot of books, shoes, and who knows what else to create such a strong smell so fast. The mall's underground storage facilities had a ventilation system as old as the mall's most frequent visitors. If it didn't dry out soon, the whole floor would reek of mold.

The gray floor was still wet, so Paul had to tread carefully en route to his storeroom. The double doors were wide open for ventilation, and he could see a crack in the ceiling, from which water was still dripping.

He looked at the industrial shelving units that usually held the numerous cartons of the over two thousand different stockkeeping units, or SKUs, the items his store sold. The water had hit four separate shelving units, so he had been very fortunate that so little damage had been incurred. He thanked the gods of plastic covering and vacuum wrapping.

He went to look at Kadence's storeroom, adjacent to his own. The place was a mess. A large part of the ceiling had caved in, and he could see the long crack in the old pipes. Large pieces of plaster decorated the floor, amidst soggy pages, wet bindings, and soaking heart-shaped greeting cards.

In the middle of the storeroom stood a middle-aged man with a mop of black hair, dressed in work overalls sporting "Al's Plumbing" in yellow lettering on the back. He was giving orders to a young man who seemed frightened by his own shadow.

"So, what's the verdict?" Paul asked the plumber.

"A deadly combination of old pipes and last night's sudden chill," was the reply. "We had a case like this in Palm Beach last year."

"I'm from storeroom A-5, next door. How long until I will be able to put stock back in my storeroom?"

Al scratched his forehead with a pencil and took a step to the right, as if the lighting was better there. "Six, maybe seven weeks."

"You mean days, right?" Paul's shock showed.

"There is no way this will take less than that," the plumber reported. "I have to break open the ceiling of the entire section, replace the main pipes, and close it back up again. If that isn't enough, the whole apparatus is so old, I don't even know if I can find joints that fit. There's a good chance that we'll have to replace the entire system. And I can't be responsible for anything left in here until we complete the job."

"Isn't there some way you could complete it sooner?" Paul was deeply concerned.

"Afraid not," Al answered, and then added, "I'm in the middle of another three projects as it is. I dropped everything to get here, and god knows what other emergency will pop up before we finish this job."

"But Thursday is Valentine's Day!" Paul said desperately. "I need to have an operational storeroom!"

"Oh, thanks for reminding me," the plumber said. "I really should pick up some roses for my wife."

Paul bounded up the stairs, furious, and burst into the mall manager's office, only to find three other store managers yelling at Raul.

"I don't have any more free space!" Raul claimed in desperation. "Kaffee Books and Eleganz Shoes were hit the worst, so I gave them the two areas I had."

"So what are you doing about the situation?" Jimenez, the hardware store manager, demanded angrily.

"We're fixing the pipes. It's all I can do. The insurance will cover any damages. You've got nothing to worry about." The mustachioed mall manager sounded like he was quoting a manual.

"It's not just about the damages," Paul insisted, arms flailing. "We're coming up on Valentine's Day—I can't afford to lose the sales!"

"There's nothing I can do about that," Raul said. "But any damages will be covered. Any damages."

Paul left Raul's office frustrated. No solution had been offered and he had to open the store; if not today, then at the latest, tomorrow. But what could he do with his stock? Where could he put it? An alternative storage space had to be found immediately.

Reentering Hannah's Shop, this time through the front doors, he was overwhelmed by the number of boxes that filled the aisles all the way to the rear. Everyone was busy. Some were unpacking damaged boxes, some were checking goods, and some were wiping water from plastic-coated merchandise. Even his secretary Alva was buried in towels.

He walked into his office, opened the yellow pages, and started calling nearby warehouses.

"You need storage space today? Well, I'm sure we could make a deal. How about twenty-five dollars a square foot?"

Three minutes later, "I'm sorry, but we just rented out the last space we had. It looks like we will have a vacancy two weeks from now. Shall I place a reservation?"

The last one on the list said, "What do you want? That's the price in Boca. You want something cheaper? I've got something in Delray Beach."

Paul hung his head in despair. It looked like he had no choice but to pay an extravagant price in order to keep the store open. And that meant almost no profits until the pipes were fixed, and there was no telling when that would be. This was the last straw; now there was no way he could improve the store's performance and justify his promotion. His stint in Hannah's Shop would soon be history.

Just then, Ted raced in.

"Boss, can you come to the loading dock? The truck just arrived with the new collection."

"Oh, no." Paul had completely forgotten the shipment. He had originally planned to use the morning to replace the display, but instead they were stuck in a crisis. He raced out to find the truck driver unloading pallets of merchandise.

"No, no, no!" Paul cried. "You can't unload it—don't you see—we have nowhere to put all this stuff!"

"I do what I'm told," the driver said. "I am leaving this stuff here."

"Don't unload any more. Stop, please," Paul implored. "Wait, let me call your boss."

He pulled out his cell and dialed the regional warehouse.

"Rog, it's Paul, I've got an emergency here." Paul updated Roger on the situation and asked if the driver could be instructed to take back the new shipment.

"Sure, Paul. Let me speak with him."

Paul handed the phone over to the tattooed driver, who listened, muttered something under his breath, handed the phone back, and started reloading the truck. Thanking the driver, Paul returned to Roger.

"Do you know of any available storage space I can get at a reasonable price somewhere near the Boca mall?" Paul asked.

"Afraid not," was the sober reply. "Did you try local warehouses?"

"None are available for a normal price. They are so sympathetic to the cause that they merely doubled the price. I should be thankful they didn't triple it," Paul added. "The closest I could find was in Delray Beach."

"So you'd have to drive more than fifteen minutes to get your merchandise?" Roger was surprised. Slowly he said, "If the goods are not going to be readily accessible, how about keeping it all in my warehouse? I've got trucks passing through Boca every day, so it should be possible to organize it, logistically."

"Wow. Thank you," Paul said, relieved. "You're a lifesaver."

"I think we can make it work," Roger said. "There's no reason to waste good money on extra storage you'd have to drive to. I have plenty of room for your stock here. Just tell me what you need, and I'll send it over."

"What—like a recall?"

"No," Roger replied. "I have a clear section where I can put your stock. I don't want the hassle of changing the ownership on the books and I don't want to issue paperwork whenever I ship you something. They'll stay your goods, just on my shelves."

"Excellent. So when can your truck pick up the boxes?" Paul asked.

"At the end of the day, around five. But please make sure that everything is organized and ready. The driver will be on his way back from a long trip, so I don't want to over-burden him."

"You got it."

Paul located Ted and told him the good news. "I've arranged it so that the regional warehouse will hold the stock for us. The truck will pick up the goods at around five."

"Wow. How'd you get them to agree to that?"

"Let's just say that Roger's a great friend," Paul replied. "Now let's get moving."

"Gotcha. I'll make sure that all the goods we brought up from the stockroom will be moved to the loading dock," was the energetic response.

"No, Ted," Paul didn't approve, "not when stock we need isn't readily accessible."

"Sorry, you lost me there, boss."

"Ted, how often does the floor staff go down to the storeroom to fetch goods—at least once or twice an hour?"

Ted nodded in agreement.

"So if we ship it all, we'll be in trouble. At the same time, how many of the items that are kept in the store itself are not touched for months?" Paul asked his floor manager. "In short, how much of the merchandise kept in the storeroom should have been kept in the store and vice versa?"

"I dunno," Ted answered frankly, "but it must be a lot. Now I see what you mean. I guess we could be more efficient."

"Right now I couldn't care less about efficiency," Paul asserted. "What I do care about is to not send off the things that we need here, but to still send enough to enable us to open the store. Tell the department managers to prepare a list of things we can afford to send to the regional warehouse, right away. They'll need time to make prudent decisions, and Roger's truck will be here sooner than we think."

* * *

The office for the manager of the Boca Raton branch of Hannah's Shop had been furnished according to the chain's standard: a medium-size light brown desk, behind which was a chair with a high back, a whiteboard to one side, a bookcase across from it, and seven folding metal chairs with brown padded seats. The last were now unfolded, and accommodated the six department heads and the floor manager.

Facing his employees, Paul White sat in the tall chair, features distinctly showing his displeasure. On his desk were the lists they had compiled of the items to be sent to the warehouse. The lists were ridiculously short. Paul estimated that all the lists combined represented less than one-quarter of the inventory that had been brought up from the storeroom.

"Guys, this isn't it," he started, holding his frustration at bay. "Obviously I didn't explain myself properly. We don't have room for all the merchandise. Keep just what you absolutely have to."

"What do you want me to do?" Isabella argued. "I can't afford not to have my stock. If I ship it, what will I sell?"

"Isabella," Paul said in a sharp tone, "even if you jam-pack the shelves and overhead storage you have in your department, you can't squeeze everything in."

"I thought I could keep some of it in the kitchenette, and maybe some more in the hallway," she offered.

"I need the hallway for my carpets," Javier claimed, his deep voice almost melodic. "That's the only place they will fit!"

"Hey! Using the kitchenette was *my* idea." Mike stood up and jabbed his thumb at his own chest. "I'm putting my stuff there first!"

"QUIET!" Paul raised his voice. "And sit down, Mike. No one is using the kitchenette, and nothing will be stored in the hallway. If we did, it would be so packed, you wouldn't be able to get to the boxes anyway."

When no one answered, he continued. "The warehouse agreed to send us every day whatever we want. Let me stress it again. Because of our crisis, and as long as we can't use our storeroom, Roger, our friendly neighborhood manager of the regional warehouse, committed to ship every day whatever we need. So what we need to hold is only what we expect to sell right away. There is no need to hold mountains of inventory in the store right now."

"What do you mean by 'what we expect to sell right away'?" Fran asked suspiciously.

Paul had to think about it for a moment before answering. "Whatever we ask for during the day, we'll get the next morning. So actually, what we need to hold is just what we expect to sell in one day."

Mike threw his hands up. "I have no idea what I will sell today."

"Today we'll sell nothing," Ted said bitterly. Turning to Paul, he continued. "I can print out from the computer the average daily sales of each SKU. I don't believe that *that's* all you want to leave in the store?"

Before Paul could answer, Mike exploded, "Averages are nonsense. One day you can sell nothing, the next a ton. If I don't have enough merchandise, I won't be able to sell anything, even on the good days. You'll hold averages and this store's sales will be flushed down the toilet for sure."

The rest of the managers chimed in. Maria, who managed the bathroom textiles department, cried, "Most days I don't sell even a single chartreuse full-size bath towel, but once I sold forty in one day!"

"Forty?" Paul was amazed. "That's miles beyond your daily average. How often does that happen? How often do you sell even twenty of them in one day?"

"It happened once, about a year ago, but it could happen again at any time," she said defensively. Even though Maria was the smallest staff member, her opinions were always expressed the loudest.

"You can't act based on something that happens once in a blue moon." Paul was firm. "That's submitting to hysteria."

The debate continued for a long while. Finally, the department managers pressed Paul into an agreement to hold, from each SKU, an amount equal to twenty times the daily average sales. As far as Paul could see, hysteria had won the debate, but he lacked the strength to go on arguing. He had not had a thing to eat since he had woken up that morning, and it was taking its toll.

When the department managers filed out, Ted stayed behind. "Don't you have something to do?" Paul snapped at him. "They're waiting for you to print out their daily sales averages."

"Right away, boss, but I have just one question. The warehouse has always sent us whole cartons, but you're talking about asking for individual items. Will they do that for us? Are they even capable of doing it?"

Reminding himself once again not to underestimate his floor manager, Paul said, "You're right, I missed that. Let me check with Roger and I'll see what can be done. In the meantime, go generate the lists. Our boxes *must* be ready for the pickup."

As Ted left his office, Paul took a deep breath and called Roger again.

"Sorry to bother you, Rog. I know that you went out of your way to help me, and I am so grateful for your offer." Paul cleared his throat in discomfort. "But I have another problem. I can't receive whole cartons of goods anymore."

"Yeah, I know. I already thought about it," Roger said, stunning his friend. "Clearly, if I send you a carton every time you ask for an item, in no time you'll have your entire inventory back in your store. I discussed it with my people. It's a real headache for us, but we found a way to manage. We'll ship you individual units, per your request."

"I owe you a huge one, Rog."

"A lot more than one." Roger's rolling laughter made Paul smile. "For starters, you take the girls to ballet both this Sunday and next."

"Deal."

* * *

Maria knocked on Paul's door.

"Come on in."

"Boss, we're starting to do what you said," the petite woman informed him. "Shipping everything above twenty days worth means we're shipping to the warehouse not just what we had in our stockroom, but also a lot of merchandise we are currently holding in the store. Were you aware of this, or are we misinterpreting what you told us to do?"

"I know that some of the stuff we were holding in the store has to be shipped." Paul's answer could have been spoken in a gentler tone.

"Boss," Maria insisted, hands on her hips. "It's not some of the stuff. Half the shelves will be empty."

He ran the numbers in his head. The store held about four months of inventory, half of it stored in the downstairs stockroom. So, holding only twenty days meant holding less than half of what they currently held in the store itself. Maria was right, and vacant shelves were far from what he had had in mind. However, after arguing for so long that twenty days was hysterical, he did not want to reopen that argument. In any case, until the storeroom was operational once more, Roger would send whatever Paul requested daily. Therefore it wasn't really necessary to hold even one month of inventory.

"Stick to the plan," he said firmly. "We agreed to hold only twenty times the average daily sales, so twenty it is. Whatever is left, spread nicely on the shelves to give the store a decent look."

"Okay, you're the boss."

A few seconds after she left, Paul overheard Maria say to Ted in the kitchenette something that sounded a lot like, "el jefe es loco," and as his loyal floor manager tried to calm Maria down, Paul hoped she was wrong.

Chapter 5

The lights in the large downtown Miami building that housed the headquarters of Hannah's Shop were shutting off, one by one, as if the building was shutting its eyes as night fell. Walking down the corridor on the top floor, Caroline felt the emptiness and longed to be home with her husband and children. If her father had his way, and made her president, she would have to get used to this feeling. Peeking through the heavy double doors to Henry's office, she saw him studying a report in green binding. She knocked softly, so as not to startle him.

"Dad, do you have a minute?"

"No, but I'll listen anyway," the balding man smiled, putting the report down onto his large desk. The reds and browns that made up his office complemented his presence well.

"Did you hear about Leon's?" Caroline asked as she sat down in a mahogany chair opposite Henry. Leon's was a manufacturer of bedding ensembles based in Georgia.

"I heard that they're in trouble, nothing more."

"I recently spoke with Jason Hodge, Leon's youngest," she reported. "Apparently he and his brothers decided not to pour more money into the company."

"That's a pity. I knew Leon for many years. He would never have allowed this to happen, bless his soul," Henry remarked, and issued a sigh. Leon Hodge had succumbed to a heart attack two years earlier. "You know, dear, that when I started, everything that we bought was made in the U.S. of A. Now, almost nothing is. Well, there goes another one."

"It's too early to write them off," Caroline objected.

"Leon's is a good company. With their excellent quality and designs, it's likely that they will continue to operate under a new owner."

Henry waved his hand. "Who today would buy a bottomless pit?"

"Maybe we should?"

Henry narrowed his eyes. "Tell me more, my girl."

Caroline smiled. Ever since she was a little girl, her father had called her "my girl" when she managed to surprise him in a good way. She moved to his side of the table and her fingers danced over the keyboard. "Here are the financial statements from Leon's for the last five years."

"So, you did some homework." Henry was apparently pleased. "Where did you get your information from?"

"From Jason," Caroline answered curtly, and sat back down, waiting for her father to review the documents. His eyes scanned the screen, and when they stopped he asked, "How come sales deteriorated so much, so quickly?"

"I've known the Hodge brothers since I was little, and they never got along. From my interaction with them this past year, I know that hasn't changed. Since the old man died, they spend more time on power struggles, on who is in charge of what, than on running their business. When I ask for a quote, can you believe that all three brothers have to approve any proposal? Everything takes forever; it's getting impossible to work with them."

This was the worst nightmare of anyone who established his own company, Henry surmised. That your own children would reduce to rubble everything you had built was a tragedy. At least with Caroline he had no fear of that. He nodded his head as Caroline pushed on. "Dad, I think we have a great opportunity here. I think that we can easily turn Leon's, almost immediately, into a profitable asset for us."

"How?" Henry encouraged her to continue.

Caroline was well prepared. She answered confidently, "Right now we are their largest customer; we constitute forty percent of their sales. But for us, they're a relatively small supplier. Less than six percent of our bedding products are Leon's. If we double our acquisitions from them, even if I lower our purchase price by five percent, it will swing them into the black. Open the other document in the folder to see the calculations."

"No need." Henry took his hand off the mouse, and turned the screen away. "With forty percent gross margins, it's obvious that such an increase in sales will solve their financial problems. But, my girl, what about the good ole rule of sticking to what you know, plain and simple? We sell textiles, we don't manufacture them. We don't really know much about the complicated process of designing products, not to mention the production processes."

"We don't, but Jason does," Caroline answered firmly. "He grew up in the business, and his father trained him well."

"I'm sure he did. So you've discussed it with him, and…?" Her father raised an eyebrow.

"And he is willing, not just willing but actually eager, to continue as the president of Leon's. Provided, of course, that his brothers will be out of the picture. I think, that for a reasonable salary and modest bonuses, we can sign him to a five-year contract."

"You have covered this aspect well, but why are you so confident that we can, on an ongoing basis, sell twice the amount that we currently do? I would hate to be stuck with more surpluses that we'd have to dump through our outlets."

Caroline paused for a moment and then said, "If I was absolutely sure that it was no problem to sell them, I would have doubled the quantities a long time ago. Here is where I need your help, Daddy. You'll have to help me convince Christopher to provide these products with better and larger display space within our stores."

"Hmm…" was the response. "And who will supervise that company? To whom will Jason report? They are much too small to report directly to the president."

"I haven't thought about it," Caroline admitted. "Jason can report to either the EVP of operations or of purchasing. I'm willing to take on that additional burden."

"Wouldn't it be a major distraction for you? Don't rush to answer. Take into account that you'd have to know that company inside and out. You'd be the one to fight for the additional investments they'd need. You'd be the one to ensure that they had the right growth strategy. Caroline, do you think that you should devote so much time to something that represents about ten percent of just one product family out of so many? Keep in mind that Leon's focus should not only be on what concerns Hannah's Shop. It should not be dependent on us as its only client."

"Why not?" his daughter countered aggressively.

"Isn't it time that Hannah's Shop started to have its own brand products? Many chains have their own brand products on which they do larger margins. I checked, and yes, there are cases where chains lost money on such endeavors, but in most cases they did increase profitability. Don't you think that now, when competition is fiercer than ever, we should start to explore it?"

The president of the largest home textiles chain in the Southeast leaned backwards, brooding, and put both hands behind his head.

This lack of a response provoked Caroline to declare, "I'm convinced that we should grab this golden opportunity and immediately buy Leon's."

Henry was familiar with his daughter's temperament. He knew that the best medicine would be patience and an even tone. As future president of the company, there were a few things she would have to acknowledge and absorb. Therefore, after a short while he said quietly, "Caroline, hear me out. I think that you have the killer instinct that every good businessman has to have. You've also learned how to prepare a persuasive case and argue it using your ability to think on your feet. You've just demonstrated it—you convinced me that it's time to reexamine our policy about having our own brand products. And I agree that Leon's is a good company that has the right products, and that we could easily turn it into a good asset. But…"

"But your decision is that we will not buy Leon's," Caroline completed his sentence.

"Correct."

"Why?" she inquired in a defeated tone. All her preparation had been swept aside with his one-word response. She could feel the air escaping from her balloon.

"Think about what we've just discussed. Acquiring Leon's makes sense only within a broader strategy of developing our own brand products. But that strategy requires us to provide answers to many important questions. First, we must make sure that we don't create confusion in the trenches, confusion that will eventually come back to us as conflicts that will consume our time and attention. Therefore, we have to determine the guidelines of the split of displays between the brand products and the regular products. And we have to decide on the organizational structure; not such a trivial question, as you've surely noticed."

"That shouldn't take too long," was Caroline's response. If that was the basis for his objections to the idea, perhaps she could still change his mind.

Henry ignored her remark and continued. "There is more than one way for us to obtain branded products. If we want to avoid mistakes and floundering, we have to construct the criteria for acquiring brand products: under what conditions should we or shouldn't we purchase the production company; when should we provide only the design and subcontract the production, and when should we contract for exclusive products that carry our brand name?"

The wisdom of Henry's point of view started seeping through to Caroline. He inhaled deeply and continued. "And no less important, we have to decide on the rate of implementation, including a detailed investment plan. Caution when making decisions regarding all these issues is the key to success or failure. Arriving at prudent decisions takes time to brainstorm. Caroline, I have learned the hard way that I'm not John Wayne. When I shoot from the hip, I usually hit my own foot."

Caroline could plainly see the merit in these words. Yet still, she was compelled to say, "But by the time we manage to do all those things, Leon's will already be sold. We'll lose this golden opportunity, and an opportunity like this is rare. Shouldn't we acquire Leon's and then do all the meticulous strategic planning? We're bound to learn a lot from a pilot."

"Caroline, please listen to me." Henry waited until their eyes locked. "The most important guideline for a president is to never embark on a new strategic direction as a result of one specific opportunity, no matter how unique and promising the opportunity may seem. Opportunities come and go. Allowing opportunities to impact strategy ensures that the outcome will be a zigzagging strategy. And rest assured that sooner or later the company will zigzag itself into a brick wall." Henry leaned forward to gently pat Caroline's hand. "This is the most important lesson I can teach you. You must learn to control your instincts. Don't be distracted by golden opportunities; too often they turn out to be gilded traps."

Deep in thought, Caroline stood up. "My years in purchasing have conditioned me to grab opportunities. That's exactly what I do, day in and day out. It's what makes me a good purchasing manager. That's who I am, and that's the long and the short of it. I don't think I can make such a fundamental change. Dad, you just persuaded me that I am simply unsuited to sit in your chair."

Chapter 6

"Paul, we have a problem. Your store is driving us crazy."

Roger's phone call had come a mere four days after the pipes had burst, and Paul, receiver in hand, felt his fears materialize.

"I knew it," he said. "Opening cartons for individual items just couldn't work."

"That's not the issue," Roger responded. "It's the constant phone calls. I have a regional warehouse to run, not a fast food joint. I need my people to work beyond taking orders from your people every twenty minutes."

Paul thought for a minute. Each of his six department managers calling at least once every two hours, small wonder it created bedlam for the warehouse. "I'm sorry," he apologized. "I'll make sure each department manager submits one list to the warehouse once a day."

"No, Paul, one list total. You see, I arrange your shipment only once a day, at the end of the day," Roger explained. He firmly believed that any complication, no matter how small, would always lead to trouble. "The simplest thing would be if you send me one combined list by e-mail at the end of the day."

"You got it, Rog. Thanks again for everything."

"Wait, we forgot something," the warehouse manager said. "Remember I took the new collection back? Well, I know you don't have room for all of it. But you do need this merchandise. How much of it shall I send to you?"

"Can you ship me twenty days worth of each SKU?" he requested.

"How on earth am I going to figure out what that means?" Roger laughed. Like all store managers, he figured, Paul saw things from only one direction—that of the store manager. "You'll have to be a little more specific than that."

Paul realized that there was really no way for Roger to know what his days' sales were. He made a quick calculation. "Send me a tenth of the original orders."

"No problemo, pal."

"Thanks Rog. And thank you for bringing it up."

*   *   *

Paul sat in his office, reviewing the lists his department heads had composed before he sent them to Roger. He could make neither heads nor tails of these lists. Clearly, there was no correlation between the amounts needed for the immediate future and what the department heads had submitted. If he approved them all, the store would soon be flooded with boxes of merchandise again. He got on the PA system and called the department heads to his office.

"I was looking over the lists you submitted, and I'd like to know how you compiled them." Paul turned to the experienced manager of the kitchen textiles department. "Let's start with you, Mike. The amounts you ordered will bring your inventories above the twenty-day mark."

"But there are things I didn't order at all," Mike explained. "In the end, it'll even out."

"That doesn't explain how you decided what to order, nor how much," Paul noted.

"Well, I looked at the shelves, and it looks like there's a lot of room, so I'm ordering to fill them," he answered honestly.

"Oh, I see," Paul answered. Starting to feel annoyed, he moved on to the bespectacled woman seated next to Mike. "Janine, that's a lot of tablecloths," he said. She had asked for twenty each of a rainbow of tablecloths, despite the fact that most colors were selling at a rate of one item a day.

"Today the red tablecloths were flying, and I wanted to be sure I wouldn't run out of them tomorrow," she said.

"I'm glad to see that red is selling well. But how are the other colors moving?"

"I sold three blue tablecloths and two green," she replied. "I just want to be sure I won't run out of them, either."

"But you still have about twenty units of each color. Why did you order so many extra? What's the logic in that?"

He waved off her reply impatiently and turned to Fran. Hers was the smallest list by far, and her numbers had not been rounded up. Three of one item, six of another. "How did you arrive at these numbers?"

"I counted how much I had left, and subtracted it from the twenty-day figures."

"You are an angel of order in this chaos," he complimented his employee. "This is the right way to work. I want everyone to do what Fran did."

"Paul, you aren't expecting me to do that every day, are you?" Fran was clearly upset. "It took me almost two hours! It took time away from helping customers, too!"

"Does this mean a full inventory count?" asked Javier. "That would take hours!"

"Are you going to pay for the overtime?" Maria chimed in.

"Sorry for saying this, boss," Ted said, "but a full inventory count every day will take way too much time. Isn't there some other way?"

"You're right, Ted. There must be another, better solution," Paul said, and paused to reflect on what Fran had done. How had she arrived at her list? First she had taken the twenty-day target, and then she counted her full inventory at the end of the day, and subtracted the one from the other.

Paul laughed aloud, to the astonished looks of his staff, when he realized that what Fran had done was just an elaborate way of reconstructing the amounts sold during the day, information accessible at the touch of a button.

"I'm sorry," he apologized. "It's been a long day, and Fran just helped me figure out what we need. All we need is the daily sales, which is the merchandise that left the shop, and that's the merchandise we have to bring back from the warehouse. You no longer have to create lists for Roger. The computer will produce the list of items sold each day. You can go back to work, thanks for coming in."

While the other department heads rose from the uncomfortable folding chairs, Maria stayed seated. She did not seem so happy with the outcome.

"But what about the stuff we're sold out of and someone asks for?" she asked. "Just half an hour ago someone asked me for some bathrobes we haven't had for a while, and walked out without buying anything."

Maria always has to have the last word, Paul thought to himself, but instead said, "Good point, Maria. Each of you should make a list of these items, and we'll add them to the request sent to the warehouse. We'll order a quantity equal to twenty days' worth. Sound good to you?"

He knew they wouldn't get these items. The store had open orders for each of the items she was referring to. And if the store didn't have them, it was because the regional warehouse didn't have them either. But why argue?

"Sounds good to me, boss," Maria smiled, reflecting the ease of tension in Paul's office.

Paul was happy that this time she had not used the word *loco*.

Chapter 7

The television in the den was on. Paul's attention was divided between the large screen and the sports section of the Miami Herald. He had planted his feet on the fading ottoman and the rest of his body on the comfy loveseat Caroline had picked out for their anniversary last year. He drank the last drop from his beer, and was about to get himself another one when Caroline came down from tucking Lisa in. She sat down next to Paul and pulled him closer by his collar for a kiss.

"I'm exhausted," Caroline lifted her feet, nudging for a rub, "but happy the day worked out."

"The kids give you a run for your money?"

"We had a great time," she answered, smiling. "We went ice skating and saw a movie, one of those superhero flicks."

"Sounds great," Paul said. Usually he went on these excursions with the kids, but whenever Caroline found the time between her many flights abroad, she would go wholeheartedly.

"You know," she said, "on the way home the kids had a whole discussion in the back of the car. They argued about what it will be like when I am president."

Folding the newspaper on his lap, Paul dedicated himself to massaging his wife's feet. "I'm sure Lisa was all excited, she's all 'women power' nowadays."

"No, actually she had reservations," Caroline reported. "Ben was all gung ho on the idea of me as president. He said I would travel less. I was really touched by that."

"Did Lisa have a good counterargument?" Paul asked.

"You mean besides calling him pig face?" she laughed. "Actually, she did. She said that it would be just like with Grandpa. Home, but always busy in his study."

"She's a smart one. So who won the debate?"

"Oh, I cut it short," Caroline replied, "I reminded them that it's not the first time that Grandpa talked about retiring soon. Besides, I'm not sure I want to be the president."

This was not the first time Paul had heard this from his wife.

"Honey," he said, "I know how much you love your job, and how much satisfaction it gives you, but we always knew the day would come when you would step out of purchasing and take over for Henry."

"I didn't know that." Seeing her husband's look of disbelief, she added, "I never thought he was serious about leaving, not before he turned eighty, at least. Hannah's Shop is his whole life, and it always has been. I thought I had more time."

"We all thought that," Paul replied, silently reflecting on his own predicament, "but now that he's serious, what difference does it make? You'll do great as president." Regardless of the problems he would face when it happened, Paul could not discourage his wife from assuming the presidency. As opposed to his upcoming promotion, she would receive hers on full merit.

"I'm not as sure as you are," she countered. "I fear I have every chance of running the firm into the ground."

"What are you talking about?" His hands involuntarily stopped their rubbing and he gazed at his wife, astonished.

"My whole life I have watched my father run the show." Caroline brought her knees up, protectively. "I know I can't do what he does. I know, I live and breathe purchasing, but that's nowhere near enough to run a company this size. My dad is involved in so much more. He leads the company in marketing, logistics, personnel, shop locations, and even their layout. Most importantly, he knows when to press on and when to hold back."

Paul was surprised by his wife's low self-esteem, and moved closer to her on the blue two-seater. "Come on, Cara. We both know that mastering these fields is not a real obstacle for you."

"It's not about mastering them," she said in a quiet voice, "it's about putting it all together. What I do best is to locate opportunities and quickly turn them into good deals. That's my advantage, my talent, the reason why I am so good at purchasing. But in order to be president, you need a holistic view of the system. It's the difference between being a strategist and a tactician, and I am the latter. Just a few days ago, I got a good example of it; my dad showed me the difference between us."

"Your dad didn't start out as president of a huge chain, he had to get there," Paul attempted. "Given time you will outdo him."

"He could afford to learn as the company grew," Caroline replied. "Today the competition is so fierce, and the edge we have is so small, that one mistake of mine would suffice to start the ball rolling downhill, and I won't be able to stop it. And to add insult to injury, it would break my father's heart. He worked so hard turning Nana's small store into a huge company. I can't face the idea of demolishing his life's work. I'm terrified I'll turn into his biggest disappointment." Speaking these words, she turned her head away from Paul, toward the tall trees that could be seen through the large window.

For some time now, Paul had been looking for the right opportunity to tell his wife of his dilemma. Now, seeing her distress, Paul decided not to tell her how he was torn between his integrity and his commitments, between not receiving unworthy promotions and being there for their children. If he had done so, she would have used his issues as a shield for her fears, as an excuse to turn down this position that she deserved and that befit her. He would not be able to live with the guilt of her passing up on the presidency because of him.

Paul laid his hand on her arm and asked, "Isn't there any other solution?"

"What, like bring in someone outside the family? He'll never do that," Caroline dismissed her own idea with a shrug of her shoulders. "And even if he did, I'm not sure I want him to. Right now I am in a unique position, and if my father brought in an outsider, my influence on the company's direction could be compromised. You remember what happened when I wanted to introduce carpets and rugs? I took the idea to Christopher, who may be the only person outside the family my father would ever entrust the company to. He wouldn't hear of my idea. But when I took it to Dad, he saw the potential, and developed it into the stand-alone department we have today. I love Christopher but I couldn't work under him; he won't do anything new, he stifles any initiative. He believes that if it ain't broke, don't fix it."

"But that's one case, that's Christopher, Cara," Paul implored. "Maybe somebody else would be open to new ideas."

"But it's a case in point." Her dark eyes flickered. "The new president will not be my father. Nobody who walks in will be able to entrust so much to me. Things will change, and my wings will be clipped."

"So, where does that leave you?"

"The only option I have left is Darren," Caroline said. "Darren's the one with sharp business instincts and the strategic vision, not me. That's exactly why all these years Dad wanted Darren to take over. If he showed up tomorrow, ready to come back to the company, Dad would forgive and forget all the harsh words between them, and give him the presidency in the blink of an eye. And with Darren as president, I could get whatever I want, easily. Okay, not easily—but I *definitely* could work with him."

Paul leaned over and gently brushed his wife's dark hair. He knew that Darren's return could solve both their problems. His attempt at convincing his college roommate to move back to Miami had not fared so well, but now Darren had better look out: it is one thing to brush off a brother-in-law, but another to withstand your little sister. Instead of just working with him, Caroline would work him over.

He kissed her tenderly, and she leaned her head on his shoulder, grateful for his support. Allowing herself to relax in his arms, Caroline forgot her qualms for the time being.

Chapter 8

Paul stepped out of the service elevator, onto the mall's underground floor. Almost four weeks had passed since that dreadful morning, and he was pleased to discover that the halls no longer reeked. Raul had just informed him that the last missing joints had been found, so work would be completed ahead of schedule, and Paul rushed downstairs to see if he could obtain a date for bringing his merchandise back.

Entering his storeroom, he saw that the new pipes in the ceiling were intact, but were not yet plastered. Hearing the noise of construction from the neighboring storeroom, he peeked in.

"Are we good or are we good?" Al, the plumbing contractor, beamed.

"You're wonderful, wonderful," Paul answered, and patted the shorter man on the back. "Do you have any idea when I can start bringing my stuff in?"

"One more week at most," was the reply. "We have a test to run, first thing tomorrow. I gotta check that it's all watertight, and we still have to plaster it all up. Talk to me tomorrow afternoon, I'll be much wiser then."

Paul thanked him profusely. He was relieved to hear that soon things would be back to normal.

* * *

"Dad, Rachel's having a sleepover birthday party this weekend." Lisa buckled her seat belt and asked, "I can go, right?"

23/3/13 1/4/13 MG

"I'll have to speak with your mother, but I think it's okay." As always on Wednesday, Paul had picked up his daughter on his way home. As she started to enumerate the other partygoers, his phone rang.

"Honey, I have to take this," Paul said. "Hello, Paul White speaking."

"Hi, Paul, it's Bob from finance. Remember me from the company picnic?"

"Yeah, sure." Paul had a vague image of a chubby man with horn-rimmed glasses, sweating buckets. "Bob, you're on the speakerphone, and my daughter is in the car with me."

"That's fine, Paul, I'm sure she'll be happy to hear you made it to first place this month," Bob reported. "I wanted to call to tell you the good news. Congratulations!"

"That's excellent!" Paul stifled his disbelief. "Thanks for letting me know. I'm sure everyone at the store will be happy to hear it tomorrow."

"You're welcome, Paul," the finance associate answered. "Please send Caroline my regards."

Paul ended the call politely. It was not the first time someone thought they could gain points by kissing up to the boss's son-in-law.

"Wow, Dad," Lisa said. "You're number one! Do you get some sort of prize?"

"A big kiss from my daughter," Paul teased. "But don't get too excited, it's probably just readjustments." Although the store's sales had been doing better recently, he knew that there was no way he could have climbed all the way to the top.

"Readjustments?" his nine-year-old daughter asked. "What does that mean?"

"It's when the people in finance make a change to the worth of parts of the company, without buying or selling anything," he tried to explain. Catching her confused look in the rearview mirror, he took another stab at it. Unable to come up with an example that might fit his case, he settled for one that would at least clarify the concept. "For instance, if the prices of buildings go up in one area, then the value of the company's property in that area goes up, too. And these accountants register it as profit, although no real money was made."

Clearly disappointed, Lisa said, "So it's not for real?"

"No, dear. You see, the store's numbers will probably fall back into place next month." Happy as he was that his store had reached first place on the books, Paul was not satisfied. False success was no success.

"Oh," she said, but suddenly perked up. "No matter, Dad, you'll get the kiss anyway. Especially if I can go to Rachel's sleepover."

* * *

"Mom, did you know that readjustments can put you in first place but not for real?"

As Paul and Lisa came in through the front door, Caroline came down to meet them in the entrance hall. She was wearing her favorite evening dress, almost ready for the fundraiser they were going to that evening. Since she had no idea what her daughter was referring to, Caroline looked at Paul, who quickly urged their child away from them and into the den.

"Run along and do something productive," he suggested, "like watch television."

"Care to explain?" Naturally, Caroline was curious.

"Bob from finance called." Paul put his briefcase down and started to unknot his tie. "He said that the store was first in the region this month, so I explained to Lisa that it's just readjustments, not real numbers."

"Readjustments? What type of readjustment could possibly bring your store to first place?" Caroline asked as she led the way up the stairs. "Besides, that doesn't make sense. If it was readjustments, then finance wouldn't have called. They'll never congratulate you for something you had nothing to do with."

"Maybe it is just the opposite. Maybe Brownnose Bob wanted me to know that I owe him my high ranking. Hon, I'll take a quick shower and be right out." Paul entered the large bathroom adjacent to the master bedroom.

"The more I think about it," Caroline said, following him in, "the more I'm convinced that finance had nothing to do with your ranking. The internal ranking is so sensitive that finance knows only too well never to play with it. Hon, it must be real. There must be something that really jumped the store's performance."

"Alright, maybe you're right," Paul conceded while putting his rumpled clothes in the hamper. "I did have very good sales this month. But it has nothing to do with me. You know that sales are always fluctuating, often for no apparent reason."

"Come on, Paul, you dismiss it too quickly." Caroline started to fish for ideas, incapable of leaving this a mystery. "Haven't you launched anything new? Haven't you changed anything?"

"Things have changed on me. They sure are different now, but only for the worse," her husband called out from the steaming water. "Since the pipes burst, everything's topsy-turvy. The storeroom is under construction, so all my stock is kept off-site. With Roger sending me goods daily from the regional, I've been living hand to mouth."

"Yes, I know," Caroline said, and stepped out to try on three different pairs of earrings. When Paul emerged from the shower in a green bathrobe, scrubbing his hair dry, she continued, "If your store has been doing better, something must have changed. Your store has been operating in a weird way these last few weeks. Maybe that has something to do with it. Haven't you noticed anything positive?"

"Well, the sales are up, and since I've cleared so much of the inventory, more than was actually needed, the display is much better. Can it be that display has such an impact on sales?"

"It sure can," Caroline answered his pseudo-rhetorical question and promptly sat down to don four-inch heels. "Better display attracts many more customers to the store."

"But traffic in the store hasn't increased." Paul took his freshly pressed tuxedo pants off their hanger and started to pull them on. "I monitored it carefully. Every single day the cash registers ring about twenty to thirty percent more, but the number of customers entering the store is no different than before. Believe me, after so many years stuck in that store, I would have noticed a change."

Attuned to the frustration expressed in her husband's words, Caroline became even more determined to push on, to get to the bottom of Paul's unexpected achievement. "So, it must be that the sales increase is not because more people enter the shop, but rather that, on average, each person who enters the shop buys more," she concluded. "What could cause that?"

"I don't know." Paul signaled that he had run out of ideas as she inserted cufflinks in his sleeves.

"What can increase sales by twenty to thirty percent?" Caroline wondered aloud. "It's none of the usual suspects, like promotions or exceptional collections. So what can it be?"

Paul finished straightening his tie. "I told you, it's just fluctuations."

"Maybe," Caroline replied, and handed her husband the necklace he had bought her for their tenth anniversary. "Can you help me here?"

Necklace fastened and jacket on, the couple descended to the bottom floor of their Belle Meade home. Lisa was in the kitchen, helping Juanita prepare supper, and Ben was concentrating intently on the game console in the den. They interfered with both activities to kiss their farewells and good nights, and told Juanita they would return around eleven.

Caroline took her keys from near the door decisively, and Paul understood that she would be driving. As she started the car, Caroline said, "You know, darling, there is something else that increases sales. However, I don't see how it can explain your case."

"What is it?" Paul asked.

"Everyone blames purchasing for lost sales; if only we had bought enough of the right stuff… or if only we had expedited it. I'm constantly under pressure to reduce shortages. But I don't see how the weird way your store has been operating could possibly have reduced them."

"Neither do I, but the funny thing is that I do have fewer shortages, significantly less than I used to," Paul confirmed. "But fewer shortages can't be the driving force behind the increased sales. Two or three percent I would buy. But twenty? Not a chance."

"Only two or three percent?" Caroline retorted, taken aback by his answer. "That goes against all the stories you bring home. For the past three years you've constantly complained to me about all the shortages you have. All this commotion was about something that barely affects sales?"

Paul started to speak, but Caroline cut him short and angrily floored the accelerator pedal. "No—don't answer, it's not just you. Every week I am shouted at by the regional managers, protesting that I haven't bought enough stock, pressing me to expedite this or that. Yet here you are, claiming that it's not really important. No way, José."

"I never said it's not important, sure it is," Paul said defensively, hoping she would slow down. "Two or three percent is very meaningful. But lost sales due to shortages account for no more than that. After all, the items we sell are interchangeable. People come in wanting towels, they buy towels. If they don't find their dream towels, they settle for different ones."

"But how about sheets?" she challenged, turning onto the entrance ramp to route 195. "If I ever go to buy sheets, and the store is out of the sheets I like, not only will I not buy different sheets, I probably won't go back to that store!"

"What are you talking about?" Paul scolded his wife jokingly. "Sheets are your family's business, you never had to go to a store to buy them! But anyway, you are pickier than most."

"Maybe I am," she countered, still unsatisfied with his answer. "But you're losing all the picky customers, and your clientele is fussy Boca ladies. Frankly, I think that shortages are the prime reason for people walking out of your store without buying a thing."

"Come on, Cara, don't lose perspective," Paul said, watching the street lights flickering in the water. "To begin with, only one in every five customers who enters my store actually makes a purchase. And it's not due to shortages. I dare you to find me a woman on the hunt for a new carpet or bed sheets who will not visit at least a few different stores before actually buying."

Caroline's instincts were screaming that Paul was wrong, that the impact of shortages on lost sales was much larger than his estimate. But how could she prove it to him? She tried another approach. "How many shortages do you usually have? I mean, if you take the list of SKUs your shop is supposed to hold and you do an inventory check, how many items are you totally out of?"

Paul hummed a bit. "Mmmm...somewhere between a quarter and a third, I guess. Yes, we are out of stock for about five or six hundred of the two thousand SKUs my store is supposed to hold. But hon, sorry to say it, this is not because of me or Roger."

Caroline ignored his attempt to lay the blame on purchasing. That was not the real issue at hand. She allowed a small Subaru to overtake her before taking the northbound exit to Alton Road. "I'm guessing that the SKUs that are sold out are the more popular ones, right?"

"Naturally."

"There you go!" she exclaimed, narrowly making the entrance to Mt. Sinai Medical Center. "If you are missing roughly a quarter of the

SKUs and the ones that you are missing are likely to be the better runners, how can you claim that you lose only two to three percent sales due to shortages?"

While Caroline flashed the invitation to the scruffy man who manned the parking lot, Paul tried to come to terms with this new realization. Not totally convinced by his wife's argument, he tried to check if this phenomenon could explain his recent increase in sales. "I guess that lately I have fewer shortages, significantly so. Don't hold me to the numbers, I haven't really checked it, but my impression is that shortages dropped considerably, to no more than two hundred missing SKUs."

Thrusting the car into a parking space, Caroline couldn't control her enthusiasm. "Compared to previous months, you are holding hundreds more SKUs in your store, many of them the more popular items. This isn't just about fussy Boca ladies! These are the items your customers really want! How on earth could you have thought that this would lead to only a two-percent increase in sales?"

"Alright, alright. It can explain a sales increase of twenty percent. But darling," Paul said as he unbuckled his seat belt and opened the car door, "why did it happen? I mean, why did the number of shortages take a nosedive? All I've done is transfer stock from one place to another."

Caroline's forehead wrinkled, "Perhaps Roger has something to do with it?"

"Must be," Paul agreed. "I'll check with him first thing tomorrow."

They entered the gala event, her arm tucked comfortably in his.

Chapter 9

The following morning, as Paul walked in through the rear entrance, he saw Javier and Janine drinking coffee in the brightly colored kitchenette. He wondered whether the two were seeing each other after hours.

"Good morning," he greeted them, passing by.

Javier stopped him. "Good morning, boss. I heard that the work downstairs is almost finished. I guess things will be back to normal soon, right?"

"Yes, in about a week or so," Paul said. "Thanks for your patience. Say, despite the chaos, how have things been going?"

"I've been working hard, but it's been good," the carpet and rug department manager replied.

"And with you, Janine?"

"Every one of my customers has been smiling," the blonde who ran the table settings department answered. "It must be that happy-clappy power of positive attitude seminar you sent us to. It really works!"

"Sounds good!" Paul gave her a thumbs-up.

Continuing the line of the previous night's conversation, he asked, "Say, how many shortages do you have? I mean, in the past month, how many SKUs have run out altogether?"

"A lot less than usual. If I used to be missing things almost once an hour, I am missing something once, maybe twice a day now. You know what, boss," she said excitedly, "maybe *that's* the reason for the good atmosphere. Finding what they want on our shelves makes for more satisfied customers."

"Could be, but how much has it influenced sales?"

"Of course people buy more when they find what they're looking for," she answered plainly.

"This is definitely the case by me, as well," Javier concurred, a smile on his face.

* * *

Paul used the system to check how many of his store's SKUs had appeared on the inventory shortage list during January. He then checked how these items sold during February. The income from these items came roughly to the increase in sales. Obviously, the fact that more of these items were available in the store accounted for the large increase in sales.

He then checked the shortage list for February, and saw that his store's shortages had dropped from twenty-nine to eleven percent. Caroline was right, and Janine was right, too. Fewer shortages was the prime reason for the improvement.

And yet, the question of the previous night was still standing. How could he have fewer shortages than usual? Moreover, if the store was selling so much more, one would expect there to be more shortages, not fewer. All that he had done was to move his stock from one storeroom to another, albeit farther away.

The only plausible explanation was that Roger had been sending merchandise not just from Paul's stocks, but he also must have augmented the shipments from the regional warehouse stocks. Good ol Rog.

No, that couldn't be the explanation. For each one of the missing SKUs there was an open order; the system generates it when the inventory in the store drops below the predetermined minimum inventory. So the fact that they were missing in the store was because they were not available in the regional warehouse either. From where on earth did those items suddenly appear? Had a large shipment with specifically the items he was missing arrived in port? Not likely. What was going on?

He picked up the phone.

"Roger, good morning."

"Hey, Paul, what's up?"

"I'm trying to understand something," Paul said. "Have you been sending me items from the general stockpile, and not just from my pile?"

"Yup. Haven't you checked your special orders list?"

"You're a real friend, Rog," Paul replied. "But I didn't make any special orders."

"In a way you did." Roger sounded amused. "When your daily lists include requests for items that you know you haven't had for weeks, isn't it a special order?"

Paul realized that his friend was referring to the additional items Maria had squeezed permission from him to add to the daily lists; items that they ran out of long before the pipes burst. "But how come you had those items available? Whenever you have the inventory, don't you immediately send to the stores anything they have an open order for?"

"Depends what you call having inventory," Roger clarified. "All of you store managers, and even more so the bookkeepers from headquarters, were all over me for delivering partial orders. Everybody claims that deviating from the specified ordered quantities wreaks havoc on the end-of-quarter and the end-of-year balances. It's apparently such a big deal that the new system does not allow me to send partial quantities on an order."

"I am glad you found this venue for venting your anger at bookkeeping," Paul intervened, "but how is this related to my question?"

"Directly," Roger answered. "If your store orders four boxes and I have only two, I can't send them to you. Therefore, warehouses always end up with leftovers, residuals. This isn't a big deal for us, because by definition a residual is smaller than an order of a single store, but relative to the daily quantities you are asking for, it is plenty. That's where these items came from."

"Roger, thank you so much," Paul said gratefully. "Because of what you have done, I have considerably fewer shortages, and as a result my sales went up by about twenty-five percent this month."

"Impressive." Roger was pleased. "I'll tell the guys who have been packing your goods how helpful their work has been."

"Thank them personally for me," Paul wrapped things up. "And thanks again, Roger. To make it up to you, next time we go to a Heat game, tickets are on me."

"Can I have a beer with that?"

Not only was Caroline right, Paul reflected, but thanks to Roger, much more had happened. When he had let Maria add the items she had run out of to the orders sent to Roger, Paul had only hoped for some peace and quiet from his employees. He had gotten much more than that. These orders were the root of his success!

Shortages were down and sales were up, and Paul saw clearly the connection between the two. The Boca store's performance was definitely not the result of one month's fluctuation or of dumb luck.

Could this be the eleventh-hour miracle he had prayed for? Had he found the systematic way to improve a store's performance? If this was the case, then he had won his upcoming promotion fair and square.

Yet, strings of uncertainty pulled at him. Something didn't add up. In general, profit on sales in the Boca Hannah's Shop was six percent. Therefore, when the store's sales went up by a quarter, profitability should have increased by six percent of that, 1.5%. This would have pushed Paul from January's abysmal 3.2% to somewhere close to five percent. A far cry from Delacruz in the top spot, consistently over seven percent. So how did his store move from eighth to first place in the region?

To try and crack this nutshell, he had Alva place a phone call to finance.

"Hi, Paul!" Bob sounded genuinely happy to hear from the Boca store manager.

"Bob, can I venture to ask how well my store did last month, compared to the rest of the region?" Paul asked.

"As I told you, the Boca Raton store reached first place this month."

"Yes, so you said, thank you," Paul said. "And in comparison? How much better did we do?"

"Paul, I do not feel comfortable disclosing information about other stores," Bob answered. "All the information will be included in the report, which comes out next week. I can tell you your performance figures, however. Although the number is not final, your store made a remarkable profit, achieving seventeen point four percent. That's how you reached first place in the chain. No other store shows profit anywhere near that."

Paul thanked him and hung up. Number one in the entire chain? Seventeen point four percent? This was absurd. It must be creative accounting, readjustments, or just plain shenanigans. Maybe they had registered the insurance claim into his books as income. Maybe they had written off the lease on the storeroom for that month.

There was one thing Paul was sure of, and that was that this profitability figure could not be for real.

Chapter 10

"Hello, darling," Caroline said, bounding up from the driveway. Paul had always admired her energy. "Make any discoveries?"

"I discovered that I should listen to you more often," Paul confessed, planting a kiss on her cheek. "You were right. The increase in sales is not a fluke. It is directly tied to the fact that I had a lot fewer shortages. And you were also right that it was due to Roger's intervention."

"So you *are* first in the region!" Caroline smiled. "I told you it was for real."

"Yes, very real," Paul answered cynically, "with seventeen-point-four-percent profitability."

"Please be serious," Caroline responded.

"Straight from the financial mouth," Paul said. "Do you see how absurd that is?" Paul shrugged his shoulders and walked into the kitchen to check on the lasagna he had made from scratch. Caroline followed, hot on his tail.

"Maybe you heard him wrong?" Caroline asked. "Or maybe he was confused, and meant to say seven point four?"

Paul turned to her and said, "Seventeen point four percent. Bob also said I was first place not just in the region, but in the whole chain. He wasn't confused. Their numbers games are driving me crazy."

"Finance people don't play numbers games, not with the ranking. If they say something, they've checked it out," his wife countered, and took four plates out of the cabinet.

Paul was skeptical. "Maybe so, but it still sounds fishy to me."

"It is strange," Caroline admitted, laying the plates on the kitchen table. "I have seen stores reach double-digit profitability before, but it was always temporary. The large sales increase in your store is based on something systematic—it's sustainable. That's a horse of a different color."

"I did the calculations, dear," Paul explained, as he turned the oven off. The smells of tomato, oregano, and mozzarella were filling the kitchen. "With my sales increase, profitability should have reached five percent, tops."

Arranging the silverware and napkins, Caroline asked, "So where did the other twelve percent come from, if not from sales? I am sure you didn't cut costs by twelve percent."

"Of course not. With the crisis, I was so terrified that my sales would go down that I didn't dare cut anything that might further endanger sales." Paul frowned, bunching his eyebrows closely. "Hold on, hon. Now that I think about it, last month I didn't spend a penny more, even though my sales went up drastically."

"That's interesting," Caroline wondered aloud, glasses in her hands, "I used to think that when sales went up, there was a proportionate increase in expenses."

"Not in this case," her husband answered, donning an oven mitt. "I had better sales but the same expenses as the previous month. Not only did I not use discounts to drive sales up, I didn't advertise or even use overtime."

"So your overhead costs were the same as in January?"

"Absolutely."

"So you sold another twenty-eight percent without adding a penny to the overhead expenses!" she exclaimed, her enthusiasm erasing from her mind the glasses she was still holding. "That means that for the extra sales in February, the only costs were the base costs of purchasing! You got the full markup on those extra sales as an increase to your net profit!"

"The purchasing cost is about half of the selling price, right?" Paul reasoned excitedly, eyes sparkling, oven mitt waving. "So that means that the other half of my store's extra sales was pure profit."

"And half of the extra thirty percent in sales comes to the extra fourteen percent profit that brought you to first place." Caroline bounced jubilantly. "Now do you believe you deserve to be in first place?"

"Wow, it *is* for real," Paul said, amazed.

A quiet descended on the kitchen. Caroline put down the glasses, finally. Paul took the lasagna out of the oven and placed it on a trivet in the center of the table, as the new realizations washed over him.

He had made the store truly profitable! He had found a much better way to run a store. His challenge now was to ensure that it didn't go to waste; only if it could be proliferated across the region, perhaps the whole chain, would what he achieved be of real value. With these numbers, he knew that his climbing up the corporate ladder would have nothing to do with being married to management. There was no reason now to circulate his résumé.

He kissed Caroline passionately. "Honey, all that running around paid off. I tried to put out a fire, and I found a path to success."

"It was just a matter of time."

"Thanks, Cara," Paul said, "and many more thanks should go to Roger. But now, instead of asking him to send all my stock back, I have to convince him to continue with the daily replenishments. Indefinitely. That will not be easy. Sending me small quantities every day must be driving his people crazy. I'll drive to the warehouse to speak with him first thing tomorrow."

"Good idea," she said and pulled a salad out of the refrigerator.

"Kids! Supper's ready!" Paul was eager to tell Lisa that the first place was definitely for real.

Chapter 11

The regional warehouse comprised over eighty thousand square feet of boxes. Platform upon platform spanned both length and width, and almost reached the twenty-five-foot-high ceiling. As Paul walked through the warehouse, two forklifts drove by, each carrying large pallets of cartons. The truck at the loading dock was being filled by three able-bodied men, each dressed in work shirts and protective gear.

In the back, up a flight of stairs was the manager's office, overlooking all the goings-on of the gigantic complex. Waiting atop the stairs was the warehouse manager with a bemused look on his face.

"So, you've finally come to collect your stock by yourself?" Roger joked. "I can ask my foreman to help, if you get lost."

"Ha-ha," Paul retorted. "No wonder you're in such good shape—just getting to your office I lost two pounds."

"Come on in, I'll get you some sludge from the coffee machine," Roger said. "So, what brings you to this swamp?"

Paul stepped into the air-conditioned office and pulled out the papers he and Caroline had worked on the previous night. "It turns out that the best thing that happened to me lately was the pipes bursting. I told you that my sales improved, I just didn't realize the full impact. I'm now first in the entire chain!"

Roger whistled in appreciation.

"Take a look at these figures." Paul pointed at them. "This is how much shortages went down, due to you, Rog. And look here, this shows the sales just from items that, without you, would not have been available in the store. These additional sales boosted my profits to seventeen point four percent."

"Impressive," Roger replied. "And I'm to blame for this? That's why you came here, to thank me in person?" He wondered why Paul had come out to the warehouse. Although he appreciated the gesture, yesterday's phone call had been enough for him.

"Actually, I didn't come just to thank you," Paul answered. Treading carefully, he chose to defer what he thought might be a threatening idea, that of daily replenishments for the whole region, and opted instead to focus on the closer issue, that of continuing them for his store alone. "I have another request, a big one. Although my storeroom might be usable by next week, I think that we should continue working the way we have for the last month."

Roger went silent, concentrating. Paul worried that Roger would throw him out on his ear. He might have just moved out of the realm of friend and into the field of extra baggage.

"Rog," he started, "this mode of operations we've developed can increase profits to levels nobody thought possible. Don't you think we should continue doing it? Am I asking for too much?"

"You know you're asking for a lot," was the answer. "It takes up time, manpower, and organizing, to say nothing of the complaints from my workers. Every day, they take your list, see what's in your store's inventory pile…"

Paul tried to interrupt but Roger kept on talking.

"They have to collect what's missing from all over the warehouse, drag it to your pile, break open full cartons to take just onesies and twosies, and repackage them for transport. It's a hassle; they just hate it."

"Rog, I hear you, but—"

"Hasn't anyone told you not to interrupt when adults are speaking? Let me finish," Roger said smiling. "For a long time I've felt that there's something awry with the way the warehouse operates. The fact that stores hold months and months of inventory, yet so many individual SKUs are missing, just doesn't make sense. And I am constantly yelled at, no matter what I do. It just shows that something isn't right."

Roger took a sip from the black liquid in his cup and continued, still intensely focused, "Your idea of shipping to the store only what it really needs sounds like the kind of solution I've been looking for. The fact that it has such an impact on sales only supports this. But for the system to be truly efficient, it should be implemented for the whole region, not just in Boca."

Paul couldn't believe his ears. He had been so sure that he would have to beg Roger to help him out. The idea of changing the way all the region's stores worked was not a mere trifle, and he had thought that it might take weeks to convince his friend to collaborate. This response came as a complete surprise.

"The thing is," Roger added, "for that we'll have to get Martin's approval."

"That cheapskate," Paul inserted. He had no love for his direct boss, the regional manager.

Roger continued, ignoring his friend's comment. "Having said all that, I am still worried about the logistics. Even if you get the go-ahead, it will take a lot of changes. As long as it was a favor for one store, that was one thing, but I don't know how to manage replenishing for daily consumption across the whole region. I need more time to think about it. Paul, I'm with you, but before I make any changes in the way the warehouse runs, I need to know that these results are sustainable."

Paul asked hopefully, "So what are you saying—will *we* continue to get the daily replenishments?"

"Yeah, sure," Roger answered. "Let's keep this up until the end of the quarter, to see how it goes. Meanwhile, I'll try to figure out how to do it on a larger scale. I may get a few complaints from my team, but they'll have to grin and bear it."

"I have an idea that might make things a little easier for them," Paul said. "You said that it's a hassle to be fishing from two ponds? Just fish the goods for my store from the general pile."

"You are aware that if I merge the Boca store's stock with the warehouse inventory, I'll also need to move it on the books," Roger said. Checking to see if his friend fully understood the repercussions he added, "Do you realize that you're suggesting giving away almost your entire inventory? Once it's part of the general pile, I cannot ensure its availability to you. I am not allowed to allocate my stock."

"That's not what bothers me. The real issue is that for such a move I'll definitely need Martin's approval," Paul huffed. "Think there's any way he'll approve?"

"Not a chance in hell."

"Thanks for the encouragement," Paul said. He knew how tough Martin could be. "But since you've done so much for me, I have to give it my best shot to lighten your load. I'll speak with Martin ASAP."

As they walked back to the front of the warehouse, Paul thanked his friend and sent regards from Caroline to Liz and the kids. Driving to Boca, Paul felt pleased with himself. Roger was on board for the next two months, giving him a real chance to prove the system worked. Moreover, they saw eye to eye about implementing this new method of running stores and their inventory across the region.

The question now was could he convince Martin, the regional manager, to allow them to transfer the inventory on the books?

* * *

Paul returned from the regional warehouse both enthused and apprehensive. Stepping into his office, Paul asked Alva to place a call to the regional manager.

"Hello, Paul," Martin's pleasant baritone resounded. "I was just about to call you. I got the report from finance. Apparently you came in first this month. I know how hard things have been, with the burst pipes, and I would like to congratulate you personally. Please tell all your employees how much I appreciate their hard work."

"Thank you," Paul replied, "but it wasn't just hard work. We are doing things differently. It's a whole new method."

"Pardon?"

Paul told Martin what he and Roger had worked out. "As you can plainly see, we should implement this new method throughout the region!"

"Hold on one second," Martin said in a tone that implied which of the two was the superior. "I'm happy you had a good month. Very happy. But let's get things straight. We have a good system, and it works well. To start making any changes based on one store's performance for one month is just ludicrous. No one works that way. You may be accustomed to shortcuts, being the son-in-law and all, but I believe in established, prudent methods. That's the only way to achieve real success."

"But the numbers speak for themselves," Paul said, fuming inside. If there was one thing he had insisted on, it was *no* shortcuts. Sidestepping around the insult, he pushed ahead intently. "Seventeen-percent profitability! Let's face it, if the Boca store had shown just seven percent, wouldn't you have been happy?"

"It's only for one month. It's a fluke," Martin said decisively. "You have no idea what the implications are. It may be at the expense of next month's sales, which means that you will be right back where you started."

"At least let Roger and me continue," Paul tried navigating Martin along his path, "and you will realize that it is not a fluke; that it is a new system; that such results can be obtained by every store in the region. I'm sure I can produce the same results, month after month."

"By all means," Martin replied. "Show me that it is sustainable over a significant amount of time, and then we'll talk." After all, Martin thought to himself, he had nothing to lose. If Paul succeeded, it was good—the region would lead the chain, and if he failed, at least the Boca store manager would have learned a lesson.

"Fine, Martin. But for that, I need you to approve a small bureaucratic step." This was Paul's aim, and he hoped that his tactic would work. He had deliberately started with what his regional manager would consider an outrageous idea, knowing full well that Martin would not approve. However, it maneuvered Martin into a position where he had to allow Paul to continue operating in his current mode.

After a short—and not so smooth—debate, Martin agreed to the formal transfer of Paul's store's inventory back to the warehouse.

Despite Martin's sour attitude, Paul felt he had succeeded. The regional manager had given the green light Paul needed for Roger's continued cooperation. And Paul knew that with the new method of replenishing the daily consumption, there was no way he could fail.

* * *

The one thing Ted hated about the loading dock was the awful noise the conveyor belt made. Trying to pretend it didn't grate on his spinal cord, he reviewed the dispatch list as two of his staff arranged boxes on the hand truck.

"We're missing stuff," he said aloud.

"Don't blame me, I'm just the driver," was the impatient response he received.

"I know, sorry," Ted replied.

He scowled. Each day a few more items that had been ordered weren't sent. The list of these SKUs was now more than a page long.

Paul had been clear on how important it was to have as few shortages as possible. He would have to bring this trend to his boss's attention.

* * *

Paul rang the doorbell to the Woods' home. It was his turn to take the girls to their ballet lesson.

"Hi, Paul. Hi, Lisa. You're a bit early. Nikki's still busy getting ready." As Liz opened the door Lisa ran upstairs to see what her friend was up to. "Why don't you come on in?"

"Is that Paul?" Roger called. Paul followed the voice to the kitchen, and found his friend in a "you're a hottie" apron, cutting vegetables. Paul took a handful of carrot sticks, despite Roger's glare.

"The apron befits you as a man," Paul sneered. "Does it come in other shades of pink?"

"Do not mock a man holding a knife," Roger grinned, dicing a large onion with fervor.

"Say, since I'm already here, can we talk business?" Paul asked.

"You might end up sounding like your father-in-law if you do," Roger said in jest. "But okay."

"Since we talked a week ago, we've been keeping a close eye on the shortages. Apparently, slowly but surely, the shortages are creeping back in. Each day another three or four items are not being replenished," Paul said.

"Why are you surprised?" Roger asked. "As I told you, the SKUs that you were missing I replenished from the residuals that I had. But how long do you expect residuals to last? Especially when you're selling them at such a high rate, it should be no surprise to you that I am running out of more and more SKUs."

That was exactly what Paul was afraid of. The entire jump in profit came from the fact that they had fewer shortages. The fact that they had fewer shortages was because Roger had provided the goods from his residual stocks. But, as the residual stocks were consumed, the store was gradually drifting back to its starting point. There was still one thing that could be done, Paul had concluded. And he had come early, hoping he could convince Roger to do it.

"I was wondering whether you could get more from the chain's other regional warehouses. There are nine of them, and at least one or two must have considerable inventory of the SKUs we are missing, and most must have residuals. Can you arrange for cross-shipments?"

"Are you serious?" Roger snapped. "For the amounts needed just in Boca, I can't request a cross-shipment. It's just not worth the effort."

"Roger, think again," Paul almost pleaded. "The quantities you are sending me every day are small, but the quantities I'm selling every month are not. Moreover, the fact that you've run out of them completely means that these items have sold well throughout the region! These are the items that people really want to purchase; the high runners our bosses love so much. Don't order small quantities—grab as grab can. Whatever you can get from the other warehouses, we can sell—and sell fast—so you won't have to worry about excess merchandise. This is good for the whole region, not just my store!"

"I'll look into it." Roger brushed him aside. He was not convinced so much work should be put into something so insignificant.

Seeing the lack of commitment on his friend's part, Paul pushed on, "My store can function as an indicator for the high runners. If we ask for an SKU, and all you have are residuals, that means it's a high runner and you should cross ship as much of it as you can. Don't wait until you run out."

"Okay, okay." Roger began chopping celery.

"Really?" Paul said in disbelief. "That was fast. Knowing you, I was sure you would have all sorts of arguments up your sleeve about logistics and transportation costs. You're getting soft in your old age."

"Speak up, young man, I can't hear you," Roger laughed. "But seriously, now that you forced me to think about it, I'm sure it will not take more than a few phone calls. I mean, I'm bound to find at least enough residuals in every other warehouse. And since I'm not looking for one SKU but for a whole list, it is likely that a cross-shipment will be of more than just one truckload."

"So, you'll arrange for cross-shipments first thing tomorrow morning?" Paul asked, and moved quickly out of the kitchen to avoid a flying onion. He called up the stairs, "Girls, aren't you going to be late?"

Chapter 12

The plane had landed just before seven in the morning. Two hours later, Caroline cornered Pandey in his New Delhi offices.

"Just look at these." She tossed two napkins from his latest shipment onto the large meeting room table. "Look at them," she demanded. Only a close observer could see the slight difference in the hues. "One is yellow, and the other is orange. You promised me that your quality assurance was second to none. I can't sell tablecloths and napkins that don't match!"

Rather than arguing, the Indian manufacturer apologized. "Sorry, sorry. I promise you, it will not happen again."

"Happen again?" Caroline snapped. "Give me a good reason to continue doing business with you."

"We had some problems in our dyeing processes and had to augment your shipment from another batch." His thick eyebrows scrunched over his granny glasses. "But I assure you it is already taken care of. You will not find such inconsistencies ever again."

Caroline did not reply.

"It is our fault," he tried to appease her.

Aware of her superior position in this debate, she continued to stare at him.

"And we shall compensate you." Before she could ask how, he hurried to say, "Can I now show you the fantastic new collection we prepared for this year?"

Caroline nodded, and laid a hand on the napkins, ensuring they would stay on the table.

Two hours later, when everything was finally agreed, Caroline picked up the napkins and said, "Add another twenty cartons of the tablecloths with the flower patterns, at your own expense, and we'll try to forget this fiasco ever happened."

Pandey hesitated for a second, but then, smiling to show his appreciation of Caroline's bargaining abilities, replied, "I am most obliged."

* * *

Watching from the back of the car, Caroline was still amazed at how the once rural lands were transforming into something so convoluted and urban. Western society was infiltrating this Asian nation on all levels. As a freight train, loaded full, rolled past, she received a call from her personal assistant in Miami.

"Good morning, Caroline. What's that noise?" Matthew asked.

"I'm on the way back from Dhonsi's factory just the other side of Pune," she explained. "I am so worn out."

"From a visit to a linens factory? What did he do—sit you in front of a sewing machine for three hours?"

"I wish," Caroline joked. "At least I would have been sitting. After the two-hour drive—and don't get me started about the way people drive in India—Dhonsi insisted on showing me each and every corner of his factory. Each and every corner. It took another two hours."

"Why would he put you through such torture?" inquired Matthew.

"To prove why his linens cost so much," Caroline explained. "Last time we spoke, I tried lowering his prices; this must have been his version of revenge. My ankles hurt so much. I'm convinced his linens are worth their price, or at least convinced that I don't want another tour."

"You poor thing," Matthew consoled her.

"Still, I managed to squeeze another two percent! Anyway, why'd you call?"

"Rhianna called." Caroline could hear the trepidation in his voice. "They can't provide the bathmats on time. Again."

"Three strikes, she's out," Caroline stated, grinding her teeth. "Please inform her that they have breached contract, and that we are terminating it."

"You're kidding, right?" Matthew's straightforwardness was counterbalanced by his willingness to work hard. And by the fact that his advice on what to wear was second to none. "She is so nice. Give her some time!"

"No, Matt. Lil' Miss Arizona should learn the meaning of a deadline."

"I promise I'll give her a hard time, but we do need the bath-mats."

"Really? How many warehouses are out of stock? I look forward to a full report by the time I reach my hotel room."

"How much time does that leave me?"

"Five minutes," Caroline said, a smile on her face.

"So you want the usual: three pie charts, seven diagrams, and a swan ice statue?"

"And fries with that."

* * *

Returning to the Indian metropolis, Caroline had just enough time to shower and change before her final meeting of the day. She hummed while getting dressed. Since tonight's dinner was with a potential new vendor, she chose to wear a striking midnight blue pants suit. She had nothing to lose, and as a potential new client, she was in a strong position.

Pradeep was waiting when she entered the hotel's fancy restaurant. Somehow, Caroline felt, the combination of Indian cuisine and postmodern chic did not blend well in this case. Although her sparring partner had chosen to wear a colorful tie, his black jacket hinted that he would be focused only on business.

They discussed trends in their business over their entrées, each buying time before the real game began. Caroline had already selected some items and patterns for Hannah's Shop, but it was pleasant to shoot holes in his arguments about the uniqueness of their designs and features. Coffee and sweets signaled the time to get down to business. In the age-old tradition of merchants, they began to haggle.

"This is a pilot run, so it's high risk for us," she stated firmly. "While I like the feel of the plaid towels, eighty-five cents a piece is way too much."

"Mrs. White, it would be nice for us to have your business, but we use the best quality threads, and as you know, salaries are skyrocketing." Her adversary took a traditional approach.

"At eighty-five cents I'm not going to risk buying three hundred cartons. Give me a real price, and not that ridiculous one, and I will consider ordering five hundred cartons." She smiled, like a tigress. She would shave off every cent possible, even if she had to order more than she had planned to.

The young salesman was not surprised. On the contrary, the possibility of a higher quantity was a direction he liked. "What price do you have in mind?"

"We are discussing kitchen towels, not bath sheets. Fifty-two cents would be more appropriate," Caroline said mercilessly.

The young man pretended to be shocked. "We can't sell at a price lower than our cost."

Caroline didn't blink at his dramatic performance. She just smiled cynically.

"Maybe I can go down to eighty-two cents." The salesman tried his luck.

"Five hundred cartons..." Caroline answered in a singsong voice.

"Seventy-nine cents."

Caroline waved at the waiter for the check.

"Okay, okay. I think I can get it for you at seventy-five cents. But that will certainly cost me my commission."

"Sixty-five, and bring the matching oven mitt and pot holder sets down to a dollar ninety-five instead of two-twenty-five, and I will order a hundred cartons of those."

"You're torturing me," Pradeep wrung his hands.

"Thirty cents is too big a drop. We can go down to two-ten, and that is already too low."

"Make it a round two dollars, and I'll buy a dozen dozens of the chef's hat and coat packages," she offered. "They will complement your other products nicely."

"Done. Seventy for the towels, two dollars for the pot holder sets and ten for the chef's clothing." The merchant was more than satisfied. For a first-time deal with Hannah's Shop, he had brought in a large order.

"Not so fast," she countered. "For the quantity I'm ordering I'll pay sixty-seven cents for the towels."

"You are a tough negotiator," he said seriously, and after a slight hesitation, smiled, "and we have a deal."

They shook hands to finalize the agreement. "I'll have the paperwork sent here, to your hotel, first thing in the morning."

"It was a pleasure doing business, Pradeep. I look forward to more in the future."

After he left, Caroline stayed in her chair for a while, enjoying the evening and the view from the large patio. She was pleased with herself. This was why she loved her job so much. She knew that no one else could have gotten a better deal for Hannah's. Not only had she lowered the prices for the products significantly, she had also added a new accessory, the chef's hat and coat, which she was sure would be a hit.

She wasn't ready to take over the helm from her father, but at least she knew purchasing like the back of her hand. In this field she always did only what was right for the company.

* * *

The trade fair was a rainbow of colors, booths and stalls decorated to entice buyers to consider the wares on display. Shiny, sequined shirts; square samples of satin sheets; silver, silky stockings. Caroline had arrived early on the first day of the IndiTextile Exposition, and strode up and down the aisles that filled the large hall accompanied by the buyer for Florida Fashions. Julie was the kind of friend you saw in Mumbai but never had lunch with back home, even though you lived in the same city.

"See? We use the latest software to speed up the process," came a voice from beneath a turban. "You can take home a sample, and my details, and we'll take it from there, yes?"

"Look, Caroline," the dyed-blonde said, "they have matching superhero sheets and pajamas. Maybe you could sell them as a set."

"Stop teasing," Caroline replied while jotting down notes in her PDA. She took the package from the vendor and answered her friend. "You know we don't do fashion. It's almost as risky as changing your hair color. Let's get going. There's a lot to see, and only so many hours in the day."

Moving on down the aisles, they sought out Baruah Textiles, which a mutual acquaintance had recommended. A new name on the market was always worth looking into. Besides, she had discovered that Craig's, their largest competitor in Alabama, had already cut a deal with them.

Finally they located them. A small stand stood in the middle of a large display space. The young woman standing at the stall apologized in a typically Indian singsong. "There was much logistics involved, and we did not manage to get organized in time for this morning's opening. But the truck is on its way, and tomorrow morning we will have a full display."

Knowing that she would not be there tomorrow, Caroline rationalized: if they had such difficulty bringing a worthy display within India, who knows what sort of problems could arise when they had to ship merchandise abroad. Better not to do business with disorganized suppliers. Julie and Caroline moved on.

Chapter 13

"Paul, Bob from finance is on the line."

Three weeks had passed since Bob had leaked the good news to him. Wondering what it was this time, Paul answered brightly, "Good morning. How are you doing?"

"I'm fine, Paul, just fine." Bob sounded concerned. "Everything okay with you?"

"Yes, everything's swell."

"Okay then. Can I ask you a question about the store?"

"Sure, shoot."

"There's something strange in our listings," the finance associate said carefully, "and we're trying to find out where the mistake occurred. My records show the Boca Raton store's inventory at a partial level, somewhere around a quarter of what it should be. I thought I'd check if by any chance this mishap happened at your end."

"No, there's been no mishap," Paul smiled. "We transferred the title for most of the store's inventory, actually everything above the twenty-day mark, to the regional warehouse."

What was going on? Bob wondered to himself. First of all, a store could not operate with such a low level of inventory. Secondly, false transfer of title was practically a criminal act. These two pieces of data meant, he thought, that someone was cooking the books. However, and this was the third aspect involved, Paul *was* the son-in-law of Mr. Aaronson himself. Approval may have been given at the highest level. This minefield had to be crossed with utmost care.

"That's an irregular move," he said in response, and then asked, "so if I check the inventory of the Southern Florida regional warehouse I'll find a correlating change to its inventory listings?"

"Yes, sure," Paul answered. "At least, it should be there."

"Paul," Bob said, still feeling uncomfortable, "you are aware that such transfer of title is not in line with our accounting regulations. It requires approval from upper management."

A long time ago, Paul reached the conclusion that bean counters live in a world of their own, a world of rules and regulations. In a flat tone he commented, "It was authorized by Martin Langley, the regional manager."

"I'm afraid that's not enough." Knowing that managers tend to dismiss such a statement, Bob clarified, "I'll have to bring this to my boss's attention."

Paul did not want to ask who had the power to authorize such an act, as he was afraid that the answer would be the chief operations officer. Paul knew full well that the chances that Christopher would allow them to operate in this untraditional way before he could show sustainable results were close to nil. Bob's intervention could ruin all he and Roger had worked for. Bloody bureaucracy.

Aloud, he politely asked, "Why doesn't Martin's approval suffice?"

"Except for special circumstances, which have to be documented in full and require executive approval, our procedures demand that all inventories be registered according to physical location."

Paul's voice was slightly raised when he replied, "But the inventory is actually in the regional warehouse."

"The inventories were physically transferred from your store to the warehouse?" Bob's disbelief came across clearly. "Do I understand that the shop is actually operating with almost no inventory to speak of?"

"If you call an amount equal to twenty days of future sales nothing to speak of," Paul answered. "What we are finding out is that it's plenty. As you yourself know by the numbers you compiled last month, we did come in first, didn't we?"

"I don't understand," Bob replied. "Last month you had a spectacular month, granted. But what does it have to do with your decision to transfer the stock? According to the books, this transfer took place at the beginning of this month."

Bob was relatively low on the pecking order, but if he initiated an investigation it would be bound to draw Christopher's attention. Paul took a deep breath and started to explain. "Bob, you might have heard that about two months ago I had a flood in the storeroom. Rather than renting expensive space I decided to temporarily transfer a lot of my stock to the regional warehouse."

"I'm with you so far," Bob said.

"Since then," Paul continued, "my store holds only twenty-days sales worth of merchandise. Encouraged by last month's results, we decided to extend it until further notice."

"But that makes it a permanent change," Bob interjected. "You have to register it correctly."

"That's exactly what we have done."

"I see. So, the books now reflect the transfer that was actually done two months ago."

"Correct."

"Jeez, then the numbers are for real!" Bob was pleased to have this mystery unraveled.

"What are you talking about?" Paul asked.

"I am simply amazed. I've been keeping an eye on your store. Your increase in profit has, naturally, improved your return-on-investment as well. But now that you cut your inventory so dramatically, your ROI has gone through the roof. I have *never* seen anything like it!"

"Thanks," Paul said, "I appreciate you keeping me informed."

"Do you think you can keep this up?"

"I intend to."

"Wow, this is so amazing," Bob said, enthused. "You're still in first place in profitability across the chain, and now, with this ROI, man, I know which horse I'm betting on in the office pool."

* * *

Later that evening, the White family held an online video call between Florida and Mumbai. When the children finished reporting on school, sports, and sibling rivalries, Paul scooted them off to get ready for bed. Once Ben and Lisa finally left the brightly lit study, Paul said, "Honey, just to remind you, tomorrow night Lydia is taking us to the

Miami City Ballet. I don't know why I let you two convince me to let the kids go. It *is* a school night."

"Is Ben still pulling faces?"

"Yes," Paul said with a wry smile. "He's been moping around, saying that ballet is only for girls and how dare I not let him bring his MP3 player. Anyhow, I'm not sure we'll be able to have our call before you go to work."

"Yeah, hon," she replied, her smile spreading across the computer screen. "I put a reminder in my PDA. It says clearly: Do not wake up before eight."

"You can get up that late?" he said humorously. "I thought that every morning you jumped out of bed and ran to go shopping with Julie!"

"I wish," she responded. "The exhibit wasn't that great. Last year was much better. How are things in Boca?"

"Well, today that nitpicker from finance, Bob, called me again and gave me a hard time about the transfer of my stocks to Roger's books." Paul gave an account of the conversation to Caroline.

When he finished, she asked, "By how much did he say that your ROI improved?"

"He didn't give a number. He just said that he's never seen anything like it. I can give you a good estimation, however. My profitability was about three times that of an average store, and my inventories are about a quarter of what they were."

"That brings your store's ROI to more than ten times what it was before," Caroline completed his calculation.

"Ten times," Paul said pseudo-proudly. "Isn't that nice?"

"Nice? Just nice? Paul, it's unbelievable." Caroline did not understand her husband's indifference.

"And I thought," Paul laughed aloud, "that only accountants were fascinated by numbers. I forgot that executives like to play with them as well."

"Paul, don't you realize how important this is?" Caroline was surprised.

"Frankly, I don't," Paul admitted. "I don't see any reason to get excited. Let me finish, dear. The profit increase is real, but that is not the case for the reduction of inventories."

"What do you mean?" Caroline said, puzzled. "Didn't you just say your store's ROI is ten times higher than any other store we have?"

"Yes, it is," Paul answered. "So what?"

"But look at how important it is," Caroline argued. "Look at the global picture..."

"If you look at the global picture, dear, the stock that was removed from my store is now sitting in Roger's warehouse. The value of the merchandise merely moved from one pocket of the company to another, so the company's ROI stays the same. I don't get why you're so excited."

"Paul, take my word for it that at corporate, return-on-investment is even more important than profit."

"If you say so, dear."

Caroline saw that she had gained no ground with her husband. If she could have, she would have reached through the computer screens and given her husband a good shake. "Why am I getting excited? Because this increase in ROI is as important as the increase in your sales. It has huge ramifications on how fast the chain can be expanded."

And then, in almost a pleading tone, trying to get across to her stubborn husband, she added, "Paul, don't you see that your store's performance decisively demonstrates that a shop can successfully operate with just a quarter of the usual inventory? We can open new stores with a fraction of the investment. With such high ROI per store, approving the capital is a no-brainer."

"Oh, I see what you mean," Paul said. Caroline had a good point, he thought. "Sorry, but the ROI measurement threw me off. As an operations guy, I see things more clearly when using the equivalent measurement—inventory turns. My different mode of operation has also made the store's operation much more efficient. It propelled the store's inventory turns. This is big. This is really big."

Caroline beamed through the screen. "I can't wait to discuss it with Dad."

His reluctance to use any familial shortcut caused Paul to react instinctively. "Please wait," he said, and then added, "the problem is that I can't afford to miss even one month. A bad month, a drop in the numbers, and Martin will force us to revert back. And then all is lost."

"What can you do to guarantee that Martin will not pull the plug? Shall I have a word with him?" Caroline started to worry.

"Dear, for now just leave it to me," Paul said deter-minedly.

"My hero," she said, and blew him a kiss. "Sorry, I have to run or Julie will dip me into a vat of spicy green curry. Great news. Super news. Good night, love."

"Good morning to you, too."

Chapter 14

Ted had bought himself some frozen yogurt from one of the colorful stands at the Boca Beach Mall. His girlfriend had said something about his figure, so he was cutting back on the amount of ice cream he consumed. Anyhow, the blueberry-almond-caramel swirl was scrumptious. Scooping another overloaded spoonful into his mouth, he heard two familiar voices walking toward the food court.

"I passed by the new mall after work last Friday," Javier said to Isabella, "and there are three new department stores going up. I'm sure they could use an experienced salesperson like you."

"Thanks," said Isabella, "I'll look into it. Have you and Janine found anything concrete yet?"

Ted was surprised to hear that three of the store's department managers were looking for new jobs.

Stepping toward them, he asked, "What are you guys talking about?"

Isabella hemmed and hawed, and finally replied, "We figured that with the store closing soon, it would be a good idea to keep an eye on the market."

"The store isn't closing," Ted said quietly. "Paul would have said something. He's straighter than an arrow. What's more, we haven't had a 'going-out-of-business' sale."

"Actions speak louder than words," was Javier's response. "The basement storerooms have been accessible for two weeks now. Even Kaffee Books, which got hit the hardest, has gone back to normal."

"We're the only ones whose storeroom is empty, and the only store with empty overhead storage space," Isabella added. "Paul hasn't recalled the store's inventory, and there can only be two explanations for that. Either the store is gearing towards classier clientele, or it's closing. And we all know that the merchandise hasn't changed. One month, tops, the 'going-out' signs will be up."

"I don't think we're closing," Ted said, although he was no longer as sure as he had been when he woke up that morning. "But please, don't talk so loud, this kind of rumor could ruin a store's reputation."

"Reputation, shmeputation," Javier said. "Should I keep an eye out for assistant store manager positions?"

* * *

Ted knocked on the door to Paul's office. Paul raised his head from the numbers he had scribbled on some pieces of paper.

"Did I catch you in the middle of something?" Ted asked. "I didn't mean to interfere or anything."

"No, no," Paul gestured his floor manager in. "Quite the opposite. I'd be happy for your opinion on something I'm working on."

Appreciating the implied compliment, Ted walked in, head held up.

"I want you to help me figure out how to reduce our inventory," Paul said.

Hearing this, Ted's shoulders dropped.

"Reduce it?" He was shocked. "So, the department heads were right? You are intending to shut us down?"

Paul laughed. "Shut this place down? What are you talking about? We're the most profitable and most efficient store in the whole chain! Why would anyone think of doing that?"

Ted blushed in embarrassment, so Paul continued, gesturing for his floor manager to take a seat. "But here's the thing, I know that we could be even more efficient. When I said okay to holding twenty days' worth of inventory, I knew it was excessive. The only question for me was by how much I should cut it."

"But how does lowering inventory help?" Ted didn't get it. "If we don't have what we need, it will only reduce sales. And without sales, for sure we will lose first place."

"That would be true only if we cut items that we need," Paul tried to elucidate. "You are right that reducing the inventory will not help increase our profitability, but it will improve our inventory turns."

Seeing the look of uncertainty on his subordinate's face, Paul tried a different approach.

"Do you agree that a merchant should try to increase his inventory turns?"

"Yes, of course."

"Why? We both know the answer; still, try to put the obvious into words."

Ted found it harder than he had thought. After several false starts he managed to put it clearly. "As retailers, we buy and then sell exactly what we bought. When we buy we invest our money. We make money only when we sell."

"Correct," Paul encouraged him to continue.

"Suppose that we buy at the beginning of the year and sell only at the end, we make money only once."

Paul augmented, "In the case that you describe, we have turned the inventory only once a year. Now what would happen if the merchant was much more effective; suppose he succeeds in finishing the cycle of buying and selling in six months?"

"He would do twice the profit on the same investment."

"Exactly."

Curious, Ted asked, "What are our store's inventory turns?"

"To compute the inventory turns, finance divides the store's yearly sales by the average cost of the inventory we hold. Since we hold about four months of inventory and our markup is about one hundred percent, our traditional inventory turns were about six per year."

Ted face lit up as he said, "And now, we have reduced the inventory to about one-fifth of what it used to be. And we increased our sales. Wow, our inventory turns are above thirty a year. Soon we'll reach numbers only a supermarket has."

"Yes, Ted," Paul answered. He smiled to see Ted practically jump out of his chair. "We are now running the most efficient store of the whole chain. But I think we can still improve. We still carry a lot of excess inventory."

"But boss, we can increase our inventory turns without getting the entire sales staff so upset." Ted could clearly see how Paul's idea would meet resistance; resistance he would have to deal with. "Let's raise sales, instead of lowering inventory."

"How?" Paul shot back. "And don't tell me we need to launch another costly promotion. Our increase in profits happened because we did *not* increase expenses."

"I'm not talking about increased expenses. I want us to reduce shortages even further."

"How can we do that?" Paul asked. "Thanks to Roger, we have almost no shortages. We've milked that cow dry, so to speak."

Choosing his words carefully, the floor manager said, "Uh, boss, you say that we have almost no shortages. But to be honest, we still have quite a few."

"Yes of course," Paul waved his hand in dismissal. "Of course we have shortages of the SKUs that Roger doesn't have in stock, but we can't do anything about them."

"I'm not talking about those. I'm talking about SKUs for which Roger has plenty of inventory."

His face expressing disbelief, Paul signaled him to continue. "Go on."

Ted took a deep breath and spelled it out. "Every day we run out of quite a few SKUs, which means we can't sell any more of them until they arrive the following day. On some we run out even before lunch."

"What? You're telling me now that we frequently run out of fast-moving SKUs? Why didn't anyone say anything?"

"To be honest, sir, they may be a little wary of reporting it to you, considering the last meeting we held on the subject," Ted answered.

Paul didn't rush to react. He leaned back and rolled Ted's words around in his head. How could they have sold out twenty days' worth of an SKU in one day? And how could that have happened repeatedly? Finding no answer, he asked, "Is it the same SKUs that run out, day after day? Or every day is it different SKUs? Can you see any consistent pattern?"

"I don't really know," Ted admitted.

Paul kept inquiring, "When department managers complain to you about this, do they mention specific SKUs?"

"Usually they do."

"Do they mention the same SKUs every time they complain?"

"That's what I'm not sure of," Ted answered honestly. "Give me some time to look into it."

"No, this is too important," Paul disagreed. "Let's check it together. Now. Can you remember a catalog number of an item we ran out of, preferably one that ran out before lunch?"

"Yes, sure. Do you want to review its data?"

When Paul nodded, Ted came over to Paul's side of the desk and his fingers played across the keyboard.

"As you can see," Ted pointed at the screen, "for the red LP5 towels, which were part of the new collection, the twenty-day target is nine, but three times during the last two weeks the inventory at the end of the day was zero."

Paul examined the data and added, "And except for once, throughout these two weeks the most we had in our inventory at the end of the day was three. Such a low level of inventory relative to the target should have blinked red for us. But the important thing is that it is not a matter of variability. Starting each day with nine units and closing with almost zero means that the daily sales are consistently much higher than was assumed."

Ted considered Paul's conclusion as he walked back to his chair. "A target of nine units for twenty days' sales means that the rate was supposed to be less than one unit sold in two days. But actually, for the last two weeks, we sold more than six a day. Jeez, this is not an increase in demand, this is a mistake, a big one. I guess it's because it's a new collection, and the sales forecast was erroneous. It's my fault, I should have checked it."

"It's okay, Ted," Paul calmed his employee. "Our forecasts are far from precise, but I don't suppose that many SKUs suffer from the same mistake. Not more than fifty."

"Probably less," Ted hurried to agree. "I'll correct it right away." Then he added, disappointed, "But even though they're good sellers, since we are dealing here with a small number of SKUs, correcting these mistakes will not affect sales much. Oh well, I thought I had a good idea. I had judged according to the intensity of the sales associates' complaints and hadn't bothered to check what the real impact was."

"Still, you were absolutely right to bring it up," Paul encouraged him. "As few as these SKUs may be, each one must raise the blood pressure of the department managers. I shouldn't be so stubborn; I should have listened." In a firm tone he concluded, "However, it's imperative that we correct it as soon as possible."

"Without a doubt," Ted agreed.

"More importantly," Paul said, "you've just shown me the proper way to go about reducing the inventory."

"I did what?"

"Look again at what we've discussed. You just showed me that we should have paid particular attention to an SKU that most days closes with very little in inventory; very little relative to its target. We concluded that such situations should blink red, warning us to increase the target inventory."

"Correct, boss. Like I said, I'll do it right away. But we *are* talking about increasing inventory," Ted checked, just to be sure.

Alva interrupted them by bringing in a tray with two mugs of steaming coffee and a plate filled with cookies. Always the southern gentleman, Paul thanked her and returned to Ted.

"Well, it depends," Paul said calmly, "What about the opposite cases, SKUs that are blinking green; SKUs that close most days with relatively high inventory?" Pointing to the computer screen he continued, "Now take these bath-mats, the flamingo pink ones. On average they sell at less than one a day. Yet we're holding fifteen! The closing inventory for these has never been below ten units. What do you think we should do?"

Realizing where Paul was going, Ted did not spell out the obvious conclusion; instead Paul did it. "Considering that we are replenished every day, why should we ask Roger to fill it back to fifteen units? Wouldn't a target of ten, or even as few as five, be more than sufficient?"

Ted was reluctant to agree right away. "Let me run some spreadsheets and check to see if the logic always holds."

"Fine," Paul said. "Now we are no longer talking about fewer than fifty SKUs. I'll bet that at least half of the SKUs are blinking green." Triumphantly, he added, "Adjusting target inventories to be more sensible can give us the inventory reduction that we need."

It was clear to Ted that Paul was determined to reduce the store's inventory further. Knowing that it would intensify the conviction of the employees that the store was about to be closed, he tried a stalling tactic. "It won't be enough to do a onetime correction. Consumption changes over time. So we need to get a computer program to monitor the target inventories. I'll have to figure out how to do it. It's not such a triviality. It may take some time."

"No," Paul disagreed. "I don't want a sophisticated system; I want something simple that works. And I want it now."

Ted objected, "I don't want to rush it—otherwise I may well make another mistake, a costly error for the store."

Thinking he completely understood his employee's fears, Paul tried to reassure him. "Let's do it together. And I'll take full responsibility for any errors."

"When should we begin?"

"Right away. And before you ask, it is obvious where to begin," Paul said a bit impatiently. "If, for a considerable period, let's say a week, the inventory stays in the green—"

Ted interrupted, "To program this, I need a numerical definition of green."

Instead of answering directly, Paul asked, "How would you define red?"

Ted hemmed and hawed.

"Suppose that the target is nine units," Paul pressed on. "When would you feel that it's important to increase the target? When most days close with just one unit?"

"I'd feel uncomfortable when most days close with fewer than four." Ted coughed out a laugh. "After all, you taught me that when the result may be lost sales, it pays to be paranoid."

Paul gave him a crooked look. "You put the limit at one-third of the target. So, when the inventory drops below one-third of the target, we'll call the situation…red. If for most of some reasonable time period, let's say a week, the color is red, we'll call it a red alert, and we'll up the target. Make sense?"

"Yes." Comprehending where Paul was heading, and wary of the speed at which Paul was racing to reduce inventories, Ted took over. "So when the inventory at the end of the day is above two-thirds of the target, we'll call it green. But I think that a week is not long enough. To make sure we don't lose sales, perhaps we should demand that the situation stay green for at least two weeks before we reduce the target inventory."

"Every day for two weeks? Okay, fine," said Paul. "And the zone between the red and the green, where we feel we have the right amount of inventory, we'll mark yellow."

"Like a traffic light," Ted smiled.

"Yes, and we'll monitor it intelligently," Paul remarked. "We won't cut inventory arbitrarily, rather let the mechanism do it right. We will only cut inventory on what we have a surplus of, and that should alleviate the sales staff's worries."

"Alright," Ted said. "I'll get to work on setting up the spreadsheets right away."

"Thanks," Paul said as the sandy-haired floor manager left his office.

Ted took a moment before opening the doors that separated the offices and kitchenette from the general shop area. There was no way he could convince the department managers that this cut in inventory would lead to anything good. Since they were not going to ship anything to the warehouse, but only refrain from replenishing items they had enough of, there would be no harm done in not sharing the content of this meeting with them.

* * *

Three days later, during his usual eleven o'clock round of the store, when Paul reached the kitchen textiles department, he was happy to see the many customers examining the goods. He helped one or two out, and looked around for the department manager. As the latter was nowhere to be found, he asked Marco, a junior sales associate, where Mike was. Paul was astounded to hear that his most veteran salesperson had chosen a rush hour for a cigarette break. Excusing himself, he walked out to the mall staff parking lot.

True to form, on the faded bench he preferred, Mike sat puffing smoke circles into the air.

"Mike, is everything alright?"

"You could have had the decency to tell me," Mike practically spat out. "I've been here for more than twenty years. I shouldn't have to figure it out for myself after discovering that the trucks have stopped bringing our stock."

"What are you talking about?" Paul asked. "The trucks bring us merchandise every day."

"Two boxes, and the second one only half full." Mike tapped his cigarette against the bench, dropping ash on the asphalt.

Paul realized that this was because most of the store's SKUs were blinking green, so most of them would not be replenished for a while, allowing the inventories to drop. Small wonder that today's shipment was so small.

"That's not goods, Paul," Mike stated. "That's leftovers to carry the store over for another day. First you cut the stock down, clearing the overhead storage, then you don't replace the inventory, and now you stop replenishing the store. I get what you're doing, but not why you didn't have the common decency to tell me that the store's closing. Would it have killed you to have given me a heads-up?"

"Do you realize we're first place in the whole chain?" Paul exclaimed. "Do you realize that our inventory turns are through the roof? Profitability is sky high, our return-on-investment is practically in orbit. No one's closing the store! Who in his right mind would even suggest closing the best store of the chain? All I did was lower excessively high surplus inventory. We have no reason to hold large quantities for SKUs that sell at a snail's pace."

"Paul, I respect you," the tanned middle-aged man said, "but you are management. I don't believe you."

"This is ridiculous," Paul shook his head.

"Yes, it is. We are being thrown out on the street and you're still blowing smoke."

"I'll call a staff meeting, and explain to everyone that there is no reason to fear. On the contrary, the Boca store will soon become the model for the entire chain."

Mike pulled on his cigarette. "Paul, you don't understand. Until this morning, I was the only department head who still thought the store wasn't closing. I had argued this point, defending you and your motives blindly. And then the merchandise stopped coming."

Paul realized that words would not help him. Neither with Mike, nor with the rest of the staff. At a loss for ideas, he asked, "How can I prove to you that we're not closing?"

"You want to prove to me that the store is not closing? Get me more items!" Mike replied. "No one gives more SKUs to a closing store. You want to get rid of excess? So do I. But that means you've made room. Fill it, even with something we aren't holding."

"Like what?"

"We're currently holding just a portion of what the chain has to offer. You say you don't want to hold too much, alright. Bring me a little of each SKU you can. Just fill the shelves."

"Even if it's fuchsia aprons?" Paul tried to make Mike smile.

"Get me something, anything, I don't care what," Mike said in a correct tone. "If all you can get is fuchsia, I'll push them as well. If it's new SKUs, we aren't closing."

"That's a great idea," Paul said.

Mike shook his head in surprise.

"Seriously, Mike. You're onto something here. If the store holds more SKUs, we will sell more. The only reason we didn't hold more in the past was because of limited space, which now—as you pointed out—we have plenty of."

"It would be great if my department displayed a larger variety," Mike said, still skeptical.

"Not just your department, Mike, the whole store," Paul said. "I have a hunch that you're not the only one who feels the way you do, nor the only one who would be happy for the opportunity to sell additional SKUs. I think that if each department manager makes two or three field trips to other stores in the region, they will be able to come up with a good list of the items they want. And within days of compiling the lists, I'll make sure we have the items. Hopefully, that will put an end to the qualms about the store closing."

"Sure it will," Mike confirmed.

"Tell you what, right away I'll ask Ted to announce that first thing tomorrow morning, we'll have a staff meeting where I'll tell everyone the plan and schedule," said Paul.

"So you're going to approve any items we want?" Mike asked.

Paul stalled, thinking that he didn't want deadweights of extra surplus sitting on his shelves. Introducing SKUs into the store always bore that risk.

Receiving no answer from his employer, Mike offered, "Of course, I meant that if the warehouse has them in stock, you'll approve them?"

The warehouse stock? Paul wondered. If all he ordered were items for which Roger had only residuals, there was a higher chance they would sell well. But how could he tell Mike that he was going to approve any SKU the warehouse *didn't* have?

"I promise you that I'll approve at least half of your list," he said.

"That's magnificent." A big smile started to spread on Mike's face. "Let's get back in. Customers are waiting."

Chapter 15

Caroline's favorite restaurant was a small quiet place in the Village; her brother preferred the trendiest, loudest locations, preferably near Central Park. She had allowed him to choose the location this time, but with one condition: it had to be quiet enough to enjoy both meal and company. He had complied, not without complaining that she didn't know what she was missing.

The décor was a bit too loud for Caroline's taste, but her tuna tartare had been divine. Darren had ordered a simple salad and white wine, claiming a sensitive stomach. Their conversation had been light, catching up on his twins' progress in the new private school his ex had chosen, and on Ben's new interest in girls and football.

The waiter cleared away their plates and said something in French about desserts arriving soon. Caroline decided it was time to start.

"Darren, I want to talk about Hannah's Shop with you."

"Alright."

"And I know we've been down this road before," Caroline was following her game plan, "but bear with me. Tell me again, why did you walk away from the company, even though you knew full well that it would piss Daddy off royally?"

"This again?" Darren groaned. Knowing his sister's ambivalence regarding taking over for their father, and feeling for her, he decided to play along. "Okay, you know why. Contrary to what Dad has said to me, I didn't do it just to piss him off. It's time he understood that I'm not willing to sacrifice my life just to make him happy. The company has reached maturity; it can't continue to rapidly expand and grow. Dad built something big. I want to follow in his footsteps, not to live my life in his shadow. I, too, want to build something big, meaningful. And Hannah's Shop is not where I can do it. Sis, for me home textiles retail is like driving in Florida—old ladies driving old cars at slower than a snail's pace."

"And venture capital is the Indy five hundred," Caroline completed the line her brother had fed her many times before. "So please tell me, my racing driver brother, what sort of company makes you tick? I mean, what do you look for when judging an opportunity for investment? What really gets you excited?"

"When I find a company that has a real, but yet unrecognized potential," Darren replied. "One that has a solid chance to reach both high profitability and high ROI, relative to its industry. Of course, the trick is to not be blinded by risky dreams. The solid chance must be there. Something that will ensure that with proper guidance, and of course additional capital, the company will bloom."

As he talked, his eyes were shining, his body radiated energy. It was obvious how passionate he was about his work. Caroline smiled. This was the brother she loved so much.

"You need to quickly absorb the relevant knowledge," Darren continued, "and then analyze it correctly, including the weak links, the hidden factors. Because even if it looks exciting, you need to be convinced that the right kind of people are behind it—practical, reliable, hard workers, and above all, passionate about it."

Having brought her brother to the trough, it was time to let him drink.

"Darren," she steered him gently, "you say that you are looking for opportunities that can reach high profitability and ROI relative to their industry. Take home textiles for example, what would you consider a real opportunity? What numbers are you looking for?"

Darren decided to open his little sister's eyes to the harsh reality. "For Hannah's Shop to be interesting to a venture capitalist you'd have to show me that you can bring the company to over ten percent net profit on sales. And even that is not enough; you'd have to prove that you can do it while doubling, yes doubling, the inventory turns."

In a softer voice he added, "Sis, you know that to bring a large home textile retailer to over ten percent profitability is not feasible. It is difficult even for a boutique shop. And remember, to a venture capitalist what is even more important is the prospective ROI. Regarding the risk involved, we are looking for a hefty return on our investment. I'm serious when I make the demand for doubling inventory turns. Now face it: Dad, who is one of the best in the industry, is happy to improve inventory turns by a few percent, but doubling it is virtually impossible."

When he saw that Caroline didn't seem to be discouraged, he added, "Don't you see there is no way that you can interest me in Hannah's Shop? Let it go, sis." *First Paul*, he thought, *now Cara*. As if his father didn't nag him enough.

In response she asked, "When's the last time you talked to Paul?"

"Four months ago, at Mom's birthday, he took me to the airport and we had a little chat. He seemed a little down because of his store's performance." Thinking that she might have changed the subject, he said, "Do you think I should invite him to join me? I sure could use such a bright guy, somebody I can fully trust."

Caroline smiled demurely. "Something exciting happened in the months since you visited home. Paul made it. Big."

"He made it? That's fantastic!" Darren's face lit up. "I always told you he had it in him."

Caroline decided to ignore this comment and instead followed her script. "You say that for our business it's impossible to reach over ten percent net profit and to double inventory turns. Well, your friend has proved you wrong." She opened her attaché case and handed her brother a sheaf of papers. "These are the figures for Paul's store for the last quarter." As Darren flipped through the pages, she continued. "Look, Paul proved that he could bring a store to almost twenty percent profit and he did it while increasing inventory turns fivefold. Not double, fivefold! What do you say now, my know-it-all brother?"

Darren glanced quickly through the numbers, his trained brain absorbing them like a sponge.

Caroline continued to drive her message in. "Look at the numbers! Imagine them multiplied across the hundred branches of Hannah's Shop!"

"I see the numbers," he said calmly. "This is great. It looks incredible." Then he reached the two pages Paul wrote to explain how it was achieved. "Let me read it carefully, this is interesting. Can you order me another cappuccino?"

Two cups of coffee, a serving of chocolate mousse, and a slice of cheesecake arrived promptly.

But only after Darren finished the last drop did he put down the pages. The next thing he did was to stare up at the big crystal chandelier.

After a while, Caroline could not hold herself back anymore. "Well?"

"Well," Darren was not in a hurry to answer, "what Paul has done is incredible."

Knowing her brother as she did, she continued, "But…"

"I don't want you to interpret my words as criticism of what Paul's done. It's a real breakthrough. He broke all the rules without breaking the system. Maybe I don't yet fully understand it, but what I see is that Paul found a way to use the inefficiencies of the system to remarkably improve his store. But I'm afraid that he did not find a way to improve the system itself."

"What do you mean?" Caroline was genuinely puzzled.

"I don't see how what Paul did can be expanded to reach the same results on the company level."

Caroline went on the warpath. "Don't say that Paul just moved the inventory from his store to the regional warehouse, and therefore the improvements in his inventory turns don't mean a thing. You should know better than that."

Darren raised his hand to stop her. "Sis, give me some credit. It hasn't been so long since I left the company that I've forgotten the basics." To prove that he did appreciate what Paul had done, he elaborated, "It is impossible to increase inventory turns by just reducing inventory. Just reducing inventory will jeopardize availability and then sales drop."

"That's the point," Caroline said in a sharp voice. "Paul succeeded in finding a way to reduce the store's inventory while almost eliminating shortages. And as a result, his sales grew without any associated change in the store's expenses. That's why the profits are unbelievable."

"That is exactly my problem," Darren quietly commented.

"*What* is your problem? You're not suggesting that these numbers are contrived, are you?"

Darren scoffed in rejection and said, "If I understand correctly what Paul wrote, the reduction in his shortages did not come from the stock he moved back to the warehouse."

"Of course not. How could it? But it enabled using the residuals that the warehouse had."

"Correct. But residuals might be sufficient for one store. Maybe even for one region. How are you going to support the sales of the whole chain based on residuals? For that, my dear sister, you will have to buy more, and that will bring you back to square one."

Caroline thought about it. Her brother had a point. And it placed the problem in her lap, not Paul's.

"Now you see why I said that Paul didn't find a way to improve the chain; he found a way to use the inefficiencies of the system, the residuals, to improve *his* store."

Seeing Caroline's disappointment, he continued. "But, as for operating the store with so little inventory, there is something there. Of course, since the inventories that were removed from the store are still on the books of the company, the current impact on the company's ROI is a wash. Yet there must be a way to translate it into a real reduction of inventory. There is something big here. If I were you I would keep exploring it. On second thought, maybe I should find some time to chat with Paul."

Caroline smiled. She had gotten what she wanted. The hook was in. And she was counting on the natural affinity between Paul and Darren to do the rest.

"I wish I could analyze things as clearly and quickly as you do," Caroline said sheepishly.

"Try working in investments for a while." Darren tried to console his younger sister. "It becomes almost second nature."

Chapter 16

Walking into the regional warehouse, Paul felt that he stood out like a sore thumb in his jacket and tie, among all the warehouse employees. Looking around, he saw Roger deep in discussion with his foreman and a forklift driver. The foreman signaled something to the warehouse manager. Turning around, Roger waved his employees back to work.

"Good morning, Rog. What's up?" Paul said. He had received a text message during breakfast, asking him if he could stop by on his way to work.

"Come, let me show you." Roger led his friend across to an enclosure, which was organized differently than the rest of the warehouse. Firstly, the shelves were loaded just higher than Paul's head. Secondly, a long table stood in the middle of the enclosure.

"Ah! I see!" Paul exclaimed. "Boxes! What a surprise! And to find them here, in a warehouse of all places!"

Roger smiled. "Yes, Sherlock, these are the boxes that hold your store's inventory."

"I thought you were going to move it in with the rest of your stock," Paul said, quite surprised.

"When I discussed it with the warehouse staff," Roger explained, "they asked me to leave things as is, claiming it would be better this way."

Paul did not understand. After all, he had worked hard to obtain Martin's approval for transferring the stock on the books, with the explicit purpose of making things easier for the warehouse staff. "Didn't we agree it would be a hassle for them?"

"Relative to dealing with whole cartons, handpicking *is* a major hassle," Roger explained. "But as the guys I had designated for this role said, it would be much more of a hassle if they had to do the unpacking, handpicking, and repacking with the forklifts in the middle of the aisles. With all the stock for your store shelved in one, concentrated area, it is much more manageable."

"And this is what you wanted to show me? That you didn't need the latitude of merging my stock into the general pile?" Paul asked. "Thanks for the field trip, but you could have informed me by phone. I would've understood."

"Bear with me. I called you because we have a big problem," Roger continued. "As you know, I've been thinking hard about how to manage daily replenishments for all ten stores in the region. My starting point was that it would be a good idea to emulate the successful way I've been supplying your store. I'll place the stock retrieved from each store in a separate enclosure. Ten separate enclosures, one per store, each similar to this one."

"And after toying with this idea for quite some time you reached the conclusion that you don't have enough space." Paul was concerned.

"That's only part of the problem," Roger replied. "Yesterday I realized that I have a much bigger problem. Frankly, I'm stuck."

"What happened yesterday?"

"We worked on the list your staff put together, the list of one hundred new SKUs for your store. Preparing the shipment took us until the middle of the night."

"I'm sorry," Paul apologized. "That was hardly my intention. If it's that time consuming, I won't add so many new SKUs to the store in one go. It's no problem to spread it over a few days. If we add only twenty SKUs a day my staff will still be happy. Are twenty a day too much?"

"Paul, will you please hold your horses? Listen, please." When he was sure he had Paul's full attention, he continued. "Currently, if I've sent a particular SKU to a store, I will send again the same SKU only after about four months. To save you the calculations, it means that my forklifts have to retrieve from the shelves about two hundreds pallets per day. Yesterday, when the forklifts had to retrieve three hundred SKUs I realized what would happen if we had to service all the stores on a daily basis. The problem is not just space; the problem is the forklift capacity."

That was a little too fast for Paul. Seeing the puzzled expression on his face, Roger decided to skip the part of how he discovered the problem exists, and rather explain the problem itself. "Paul, when I have the ten enclosures, one for each store, I'll still have to maintain a general storage space."

"Why?" Paul asked. "Why can't you divide all your stock among the ten enclosures? It will also provide you with the additional space you need."

"Think again," Roger said. "For many SKUs there isn't enough stock to pre-allocate to each enclosure. Those SKUs I'll have to keep in one place. Otherwise, in no time, I'll be constantly moving inventory from one enclosure to another. That's too much of a mess."

"How many SKUs are we talking about?" Paul tried to minimize the problem.

"Do the calculation yourself," Roger answered. "Remember, for each SKU that a shop doesn't have enough inventory of, the system already issued an order. The fact that it is still missing in the store indicates that for those SKUs I have just residuals."

Paul did the calculation in his head. Shortages account for about thirty percent of the SKUs. Roger holds about five thousands SKUs. "For about fifteen hundred SKUs you hold just residual stock," Paul concluded.

"Now you see the problem?" Roger asked. "Do you understand what it means to move so many SKUs a day? The forklifts cannot possibly do it, even if we could triple the number of hours in a day."

"How about adding forklifts and manpower?" Paul proposed. "Once Martin sees my store's figures, when projected for ten branches, no matter what you need he'll approve it!"

"As far as I'm concerned, he could approve World War Three." Roger threw one arm up to emphasize his point. "I don't have room for that many forklifts to maneuver around in here!"

"So what can we do now? I won't accept that there is no solution to this problem."

"Me neither," Roger said, "but I'm stuck. I've been thinking about it since I woke up this morning. Maybe we can use different equipment.

Some warehouses that need to ship small quantities use order-pickers rather than forklifts. Each of those babies can retrieve fifty different individual boxes an hour."

"So what's the problem?" Paul said, relieved. "If push comes to shove I'm sure we can get you the budget." Then more cautiously he asked, "How much do they cost?"

"It's not the investment I'm worried about," Roger answered. "To operate such equipment, the whole warehouse has to be arranged differently. Even the space between the shelves will have to be altered. Paul, it would be like running a completely different type of operation. I'm not sure I know how to run it."

"Maybe the change doesn't have to be so big," Paul tried to comfort his friend. "Do you know of any warehouses that use both forklifts and order-pickers?"

"To be relevant," Roger said cautiously, "we have to find one that has a similar situation to ours. It must be a large operation that has a large number of SKUs but also deals with many small-sized deliveries."

Both Paul and Roger searched for an answer. After a short silence, Roger said, "I'm still a bit too distraught to think straight. You go to Boca, I'll go back to work. Whoever thinks of an idea first lets the other know."

Paul was deep in thought on the drive back. Without a proper logistic solution, his new method couldn't be implemented. What a shame.

As he pulled into his parking spot behind the old mall, his cell phone twittered. He opened the message that arrived from Roger.

"Books," it read, with a frowning emoticon.

* * *

An hour and thirty-five minutes later, Paul was in Hallandale. Roger was already standing outside a large warehouse bearing the familiar smiling alligator logo of Gator State Publishing.

"How did you think of books?" Paul asked his friend.

"Since I was drawing blanks, I decide to see who I knew, and look for inspiration there," Roger answered. "I went through my e-mail contacts and came across Jack's name. He runs GSP's warehouse. When I thought about books, I realized that bookstores hold an enormous amount of SKUs, easily twenty thousand different titles. With every new title they publish, they probably send whole pallets to the chains' warehouses. But, at the same time, for the ongoing titles, there's no way they send even a full carton of each title to the stores. One store would never manage to sell, or even store, that many books, I figured. I called Jack and told him about our situation. He confirmed that he uses both regular forklifts and order-pickers and suggested we come to see how they work."

Roger pressed the intercom button, and after they identified themselves, a gruff voice asked them to wait. A small door within the large metal bay doors opened, and a leather jacket with beard, bald pate, and dark glasses greeted them.

"Hey, Rog," Jack said in a Creole accent. "Who's the suit?"

"Paul, this is Jack Galvez, who runs Gator's warehouse." Roger made the introductions. "Jack, this is Paul White, who runs Hannah's Boca branch, the store that had the pipe burst I told you about."

Jack grunted a response and gestured them inside. The warehouse seemed to go on as far as tomorrow, easily twice the size of Roger's. Paul's eyes scanned the huge facility, across and then up. Pallets and pallets of books stacked six levels high on standard metal shelves in one area; lots of brown corrugation and pallets on blue and red racking in another. He saw five forklifts in action, and heard the tooting of horns of others. His nose was filled with the smell of paper, cardboard, and wood. This was an expansive operation, and he could not even surmise the number of books this warehouse was host to.

After leading them in, Jack explained the way the GSP warehouse worked. "We have two kinds of shipments. The first is the large shipments, to the wholesalers and warehouses of the larger chains. To these we ship the original boxes, as received from the printing house. The second is the smaller shipments, directly to the individual stores. For a store we have to combine a few copies of several titles into a box, or for smaller quantities into a shrink pack."

"This means you have to handpick a lot of books," Roger interjected. "How do you do it for so many stores without sending forklifts up and down the warehouse?"

"It's fairly simple." The tanned former biker pointed out a large area where several people were busy alongside lines of special tables, with rolling cylinders on one side.

As Paul and Roger watched, Jack explained. "Look here." He pointed to the shelves near the tables. "Here we hold a small amount of each book that is on the backlist. I mean, books that are selling. We call it the mini-warehouse."

"What do you mean by 'a small amount'?" Roger queried, hungry for more information.

"Good question," Jack replied. "We have in the warehouse over fifty million books, some twenty thousand different titles."

"That many?" Paul could not hold in his surprise.

"The warehouse for a large publisher may hold more than twice that," Jack commented, and continued, "but don't get too impressed. Most titles have zero orders for several months, so, of course, we don't hold any in the mini-warehouse. To fulfill the orders for the slow movers we use another area. I'll show you that later."

"I'm interested only in the merchandise for which you have many orders every week," Roger said. "How much, for each of them, do you hold in the mini-warehouse?"

"The number varies widely. For bestsellers, we hold three days' sales worth, about a pallet. But most books don't sell in large quantities, so we hold about two weeks' worth, about two or three boxes. That's not too much. It's all here."

"And I suppose you replenish according to popularity," Roger reasoned. "Bestsellers every three days, the others twice a month."

"We replenish when only one box is left," Jack said. "But I guess you're right, bestsellers every day or so, and the others every few weeks."

"How many mini-warehouses do you have?" Roger asked in a strange voice.

"I don't understand," Jack answered, "Why would I have more than one?"

Roger grabbed his head and started to moan. "I am an idiot," he said. "An utter fool."

"I'd hate to disagree with you on that," Paul jibed. "But what are you talking about?"

"I had the solution all along, right in front of my face, and I didn't see it. The area I had sectioned off for your store was already a mini-warehouse of sorts," answered Roger.

"Right," Paul commented, "and you spoke of arranging more of them for the other stores, so you were on the right track."

"I was on a similar track, not the right one." Roger shook his head. "Can't you see? I wanted to arrange a mini-warehouse for each store we service. Jack doesn't hold separate mini-warehouses for each individual store!"

Jack chuckled. "Two thousand mini-warehouses? Just imagine the sight. Roger, you weren't thinking straight."

"Obviously not," Roger said. "And what's the point in holding the entire store's inventory in the mini-warehouse? Two weeks' worth for each SKU should more than suffice for daily replenishment of actual consumption. Come to think of it, when aggregated, two weeks' worth for ten stores should take up the same space as four months of Paul's store's stock."

"Which is what you're holding in that enclosure right now," Paul said. "That solves the problem of space, but what about the fact that you cannot pre-allocate the residuals?"

"What is the problem exactly?" Roger grinned. "They'll be treated like all the other SKUs. The question of how to allot them has been taken completely off the table. All the items retrieved from the stores will be held on the shelves, exactly the way I'm holding the stock today. With only one mini-warehouse, and not ten, there is no divvying up of the goods. There are no residuals, just items running low."

"So can it be implemented for the whole region?" Paul asked in anticipation.

"Jack's method solves both problems, that of space and that of forklift movements. With the need to replenish each item in the mini-warehouse only once in two weeks I can probably manage with the fork-lifts I already have. Maybe I'll need one or two more, but I definitely don't need those sophisticated order-pickers. I still have to figure out the details: how many additional forklifts and handpickers are needed; how much room the mini-warehouse requires; how to arrange the stock. But…" Roger smiled at Paul and gave him a thumbs-up.

"If I knew books would make you this happy," Paul said, "I would have recommended that you try reading one." Jack laughed aloud. Roger, who felt like a mountain of bricks had just been lifted from his shoulders, joined in. The changes to the way his warehouse operated were small, practically negligible. Everything was in place already.

They thanked Jack from the bottom of their hearts and left, Roger whistling a happy tune. As his friend climbed into the company car, Paul was surprised he didn't feel as elated. If there was one thing the last few weeks had taught him, it was to not count your chickens before they hatched. He had a feeling that a new lion was waiting to pounce, just around the corner.

Chapter 17

Early one Thursday morning, just over a month after the visit to Gator State Publishing, more than three months since the pipes had burst, as Paul entered the store, Alva informed him that regional manager Martin Langley had arrived unannounced.

Wonderful, he thought to himself. The Boca Raton store's performance had stayed strong, so the tightwad had folded. Full of confidence, he opened the door to his office.

"Good morning, Martin," Paul said buoyantly. "How can I be of assistance?"

Paul invited Martin to sit in his chair, the only decent seat in his office. As he sat down, Martin replied, "As I promised, I checked up on the Boca store's performance for the last month. Alright, I'm convinced. We should try your ideas out on the other stores. For that I need you to draft an airtight document, including a full account of what you've done here."

Paul put his attaché case down and unfolded one of the less-than-comfortable folding chairs before saying, "If there is any special emphasis I should place, anything you think should be included in the official report to the head office, just say so."

"The head office?" the short man asked, a puzzled look on his face. "I wouldn't bring it to the head office before trying it in at least two more stores. I need the document to convince the other store managers."

"A document? Wouldn't a simple explanation, face-to-face, be more convincing?" inquired Paul.

"I tried that approach," Martin replied. "And it wasn't the biggest success. You see, I figured we should progress carefully, namely, starting with only two more stores operating in this new system of yours. And then, we'll see." Martin chose to say nothing of the fact that, according to his calculations, with only two more stores showing Paul's performance levels, placing first amongst the regions would be a shoo-in. Instead, he added, "So obviously, I went to the two store managers with the best performance, Delacruz and Gary, but they would hear nothing of it."

Paul was surprised to hear that these two overachievers had not pounced on the opportunity to do so much better. Prior to the pipe burst, the rivalry for first place between the store managers of the midtown Miami and Boynton branches had been quite intense. This system could have given them a good chance to be a leading store on the level of the whole chain.

"Can I ask what you told them?" Paul asked.

"I told them what you told me," the regional manager said in a harsh tone. "Delacruz's response was that as long as he is judged according to store performance, he refuses to waive control over his stock. If he transferred his inventory over to the warehouse, any other store might grab it, and he would lose out. I don't even want to repeat the colorful language he used."

"And Gary?"

"For his part, Gary said that he would never risk losing sales, waiting for the warehouse to send him a missing towel or two. He would rather have whatever he needs nearby, in his storeroom. For once, these two agreed on something."

"Can't they see that the new system brings huge benefits?" Paul asked anxiously. What was holding them back? He could not understand. "Are they so blindly indoctrinated to holding large inventories that they can't see how much better the new system is? They've been fighting for years to gain even a tenth of a percentage improvement in profitability, and this offers them an additional ten percent. Don't they believe that seventeen percent is the actual number I've reached? Don't they want the humongous leap in inventory turns! To thirty! Thirty!"

Seeing Paul's passion, Martin answered, "You know what? Instead of me presenting them with a document, how about you explain it to them?"

"Fine," was Paul's reply. "Give me a few days to prepare something, I'll bring it to you for review, and then I'll meet with them."

"We don't have that luxury," Martin said. "Knowing my star players, they will probably start spreading the word, trying to foil this plan. We need to move fast."

"So let's talk to all the other store managers, as soon as possible, before they do," Paul proposed. "We should. In the end, we want them all to participate, so why not get them on board now?" In the back of his mind, Paul thought that if he could not convince store managers in his own region, there was little chance that corporate would agree to implement the system across the chain, and his findings would all go to waste.

"Alright," Martin assented, knowing that all he needed to reach first place was two more stores with these numbers. He didn't really care which. "I can buy that. I'll set a managers' meeting, where you'll present the new system, as soon as possible, which means Monday morning. I'll have my secretary arrange everything."

Watching Martin leave, Paul sighed. Convincing people to make a change was never easy, yet the uphill battle he now faced made his adrenaline rush.

He had to find a way to convince the other store managers; something different from what Martin had done. How could he convince them to relax their strong grip on inventory and to focus on the advantages the system had? How could he explain that this way their inventory would be managed so much better and would allow for their stores to thrive? Inventory management was not his specialty, so he called the person whose expertise it was.

"Roger, are you free this weekend?"

Chapter 18

Paul opened the door to let Roger in. The early Saturday morning featured clear skies and a pleasant breeze.

"Thanks for coming over."

Roger shrugged as he entered the hallway and said with a smile, "It's all in a vacation day's work."

Compared to his house, Paul and Caroline's home was immaculate. With his five kids, Roger could only be envious of the order the Whites maintained.

Caroline was sitting in the living room, her laptop open on the ornate coffee table. Roger exchanged pleasant-ries with her, then they both started to walk toward the den in the back of the house.

"Have a seat," Caroline gestured. "Can I get you some coffee?"

Seating himself in a Queen Anne chair, Roger said, "Just one sugar, Caroline, I'm trying to cut back on my carb intake."

When she left the room, Roger, a bit surprised, asked, "Is Caroline joining us?"

In spite of the fact that he was much lower than Caroline on the totem pole, the two families had been good friends since their daughters had been in kindergarten. But it worked because he and Caroline were careful never to talk about work.

Seeing his friend's countenance, Paul explained, "I asked Caroline to help because this presentation is so important for us, and frankly I have almost no experience in constructing presentations. Do you?"

Roger just laughed.

"I even borrowed Caroline's laptop. She has all the newest software for making professionally animated slides."

"That's good." Roger leaned forward. "Let me see."

When Caroline returned, steaming mug in hand, the two men were already absorbed in the computer. "What are you looking at?" she asked.

"The three alternatives I prepared for the title page," Paul answered. "Which one do you think is more impressive? Personally, I like the animation of the third one; do you think starting with a bit of humor will help?"

"You call this ugly thing…humor?" Roger grinned. "Besides, I don't like the title of the presentation; 'Sprinting South Florida to First Place' sounds too bombastic and self-serving. You might lose some people right from the start, Delacruz for sure."

Paul turned to Caroline. "I know that this is not the issue, no one is impressed anymore with fancy animations. But I'm stuck. Everything I've thought of doing has brought me back to what Martin tried. And he failed."

"It's not a presentation you have to give," Caroline explained. "You have to accomplish something much more difficult: a sale. You have to sell your new way of running a shop; and you have to sell it not to a receptive, but to a hostile audience. They've already heard about it and they already rejected it; at least the opinion leaders among them."

"She has a point," Roger agreed.

Paul closed the laptop and asked, "So where do we start?"

"We start by clarifying to ourselves why they dismiss—" she hesitated. "Actually, judging by Martin's description, dismiss is not a strong enough word." Finding the right word she continued confidently, "Why do they *resent* any suggestion to do what you've done? And don't tell me it's because they 'resist change' or that they are 'control freaks'. If we don't fully understand what triggered such a strong reaction, you don't have a chance to persuade them."

"To be honest, I was quite disappointed," Roger said. "I was sure that seeing the results, they would realize that it moves them directly into the A-team of the company. I was sure that they would all jump on this winning wagon. But, as I always claim, no one understands a store manager."

"Mrbl-grbl," the Boca Raton store manager replied in jest. "But seriously Roger, will you, for once, put yourself in our shoes? Try to understand what it means to constantly be in a wórld of uncertainty. Remember the crystal ball I asked you for?"

As if Roger's nod was a cue to action, Paul stood up and started to pace.

"As a store manager," he said, "you never know how many people will step into the store. And when they do enter and look at the merchandise, you still don't know if they will buy anything. But above all, you never know *what* they will buy. Our forecast as to what will sell well and what will not move is just a guess...albeit an educated guess."

"To that I will agree," Caroline chimed in.

Paul stopped pacing, faced his wife and his friend, and tried to explain his point. "At last a customer entered, at last she made up her mind to buy, at last she decided exactly what she wants. Half a miracle has happened. But you don't have it in stock. You don't have the exact size, or the particular color. It's downright painful! No wonder store managers are paranoid about not having enough inventory. Now do you see that having as much as we can is ingrained in us?"

"But you can't hold an endless amount, which is what all store managers want. In order to be profitable we have to control costs, right? At the end of the day, what's important is the ROI. Doesn't that count for anything for the store managers?" Caroline asked.

Instead of answering, Paul resumed his pacing.

Roger took her side. "And how about the fact that if you have too much inventory you'll end up with surpluses? Doesn't that count as well?"

Without losing a stride Paul answered, "Will you two face reality? You can talk as much as you like about the importance of ROI and even inventory turns; you can wave in front of our noses the huge surpluses. Still, the reality is that we are conditioned to want to stock up. Every one of our shops is filled to the gills with inventory. Just give us more space, and rest assured we'll fill that, too."

"I see what you mean," Roger agreed. "But will you do me a favor?"

"What?"

"I'm starting to feel like I'm watching tennis. Will you please sit down?"

"Sorry." Paul took his seat and summarized. "You tell a store manager to send back his inventory, and from that moment on you're talking to a wall. And we're not asking them to send a box or two. We want them to send back most of it. Why are we surprised that they don't even want to consider it?"

"Apparently you're right," Roger said. "So what are we going to do?"

They both looked at Caroline.

"We have to dig deeper," she answered.

"Meaning?" Paul asked.

"What I mean is, that if you don't want to lose them immediately, you should not start at the end, like Martin did. You'd better not start by telling them the end results and the actions they have to take. It will never work."

"Yes, that I already know, but where *should* I start?" Paul asked.

"The solution that they have is to hold a lot of inventory. In order to persuade them to adopt your solution, you'd better start by getting agreement on the problem," Caroline said categorically. "And for that, you must dig deeper. You have to start with the reasons to hold inventory, the needs that inventory satisfies. And once you've reached an agreement on the needs, explain why, in spite of holding so much inventory, the needs are still not satisfied. Only then show them that you have a way to better satisfy these needs. Can you do all of that?"

"We need inventory for one, and only one, purpose: to support sales," Paul said confidently. "The real question is, considering the uncertainty in which we operate, how much inventory do we really need to hold in the store?"

"The inventory that you really need to hold is the inventory that you expect to sell until you're resupplied," Roger reasoned.

"Of course," Paul agreed. "And we have some idea how much time it will take to get resupplied; we know approximately how long the replenishment time is. But we have just a vague idea of what and how much we'll sell during that period of time."

"That's the real problem," Caroline cut in. "The accuracy of our forecast is appalling, and the variability is just too high. I hear it in every meeting I've ever had with store managers."

"Agreed," Paul said. "So, what do we do? We do the best we can. For each SKU, the computer system calculates the starting inventory. We as store managers argue, contest, and sometimes succeed to modify these numbers, but let's face it, in retrospect our interventions do not help much."

"You'll be better off if you refrain from stressing this last observation," Caroline advised. She shifted slightly on the couch and reached for an apple.

"Correct," Paul agreed. "Especially when the reality is that the system is making all the other important decisions as well. Except for extreme cases, we let the system decide when and how much to reorder."

Roger narrowed his eyes, and in response Paul picked up a legal pad from the coffee table and drew the well-known sawtooth graph. Pointing to the left side of the graph, he explained, "This is how the company operates now. This is the starting inventory in a store. As that store sells, the inventory gradually goes down. Once it reaches the predetermined level of minimum inventory, the system generates an order for replenishing."

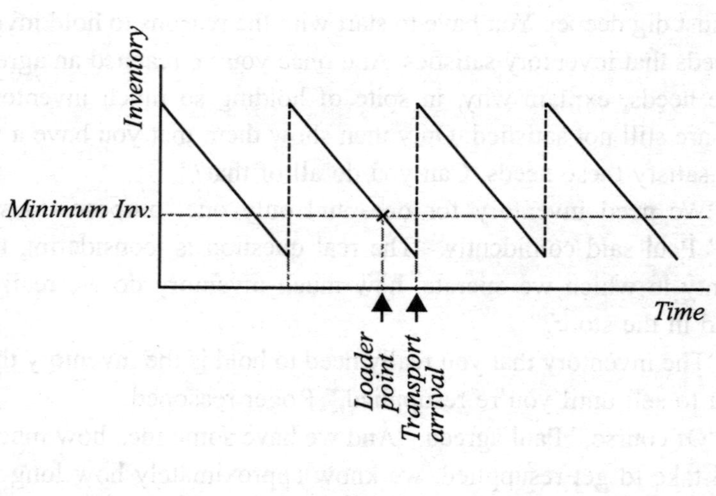

Roger and Caroline nodded, and Paul continued to explain the graph. "Of course, it takes time before the goods arrive, and until then the inventory continues to go down. Once the merchandise arrives, the inventory jumps back and the cycle repeats itself."

"I've seen this synthetic graph in every textbook," Roger sneered. "Unfortunately, in practice it's very different."

"What do you mean?" Caroline was surprised. "That's exactly how our system works."

"Yes," Roger hurried to explain, "that is how our, and our competitors', computerized systems work. However, in this synthetic graph the new shipment always arrives before the stores run out of inventory. We all know that this is frequently not the case."

"We sure do," Caroline admitted. "The store managers make sure that we in purchasing are constantly reminded of the shortages. Having, at any given moment, no inventory for about one-quarter of the SKUs means that this graph is at zero for long periods. No wonder the store managers are fighting to increase their inventories." After a short pause, she added in a low voice, "And considering the huge impact lost sales has on profitability, maybe they're right."

As she talked, Paul drafted the corrected graph. The line now kissed the bottom axis for long periods of time. "Hold it, we're not trying to justify raising inventories. We're trying to get to the bottom of the problem. Let's try to understand the situation a little better. You see, the distance between two peaks is the replenishment time. That is, the time interval that dictates the level of starting inventory we have to have. The time from issuing the order until the inventory arrives is the supply lead time: the time it takes to produce and ship."

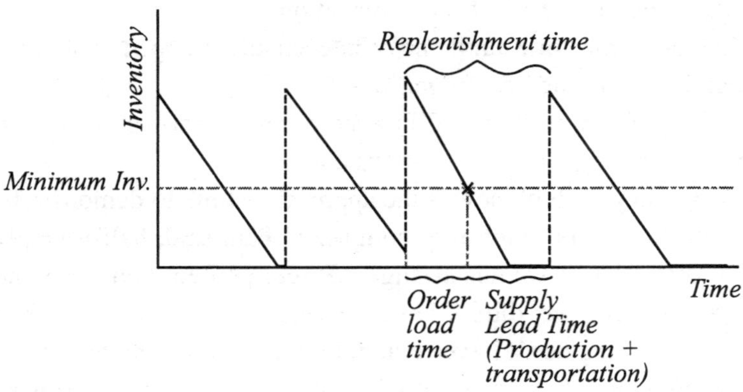

Caroline commented, "The production time is roughly three months, and since we purchase the majority of our merchandise from the far east, shipping time adds another six to seven weeks. But we hold six months on average, which means that our starting inventories are higher than that. So why do we have so many shortages?"

"Look again at the graph," Paul said. "The answer is right in front of our collective noses."

When neither commented, he elaborated. "The supply lead time is only a portion of the replenishment time. Look, I start to sell at this point in time," he pointed to one of the peaks, "but the system doesn't order immediately, it waits until the inventory reaches the minimum level. All this time, from arrival of inventory until we reorder, all this order lead time is actually wasted. And look how considerable it is: roughly half of the replenishment time."

"No wonder I end up not having enough time," Caroline said sharply. "They're wasting half the available time and I end up getting yelled at for not bringing the new batch in time."

"Yes." Paul put his hand on her arm. "But let's focus on the stores. Do you now understand why our method works so well? We reduced the order lead time from months to less than a day. I sell something, I don't wait. I inform Roger on the same day."

Looking at the graph Caroline said, deep in thought, "I see, dear. That helps, but something still doesn't add up."

"Right," Roger said. "Something is still missing. But fortunately, I've also spent an inordinate amount of time thinking about it. I think that I have the other half of the explanation."

It took some time until the White couple stopped looking at the graph and concentrated on Roger.

"The problem is," he said in a stern tone, "that we, as a company, do not acknowledge that we have warehouses."

"Rog, do you think now is the appropriate time to demonstrate your warehouse managers' inferiority complex?" Paul said, half-jokingly.

"I know that it sounds strange," Roger smiled, "but hear me out. Way back when, we didn't have warehouses. Actually, even today many retail chains don't have regional warehouses; whatever they purchase is immediately pushed into their stores. But as companies started to have more and more shops in a region, the economics of shipping a large quantity to one place and then splitting it for the individual stores became more and more evident. The early warehouses were just splitting points. And yes, there are retailers that are still operating this way."

"Carry on," Caroline encouraged him, "this is interesting."

"Once the regional warehouses were in place," Roger continued, "they enabled a comfortable decoupling between the quantities that each store orders and the quantity that is most economical to order from the vendors. The considerations of the store and those of purchasing are very different; purchasing in larger quantities has its price advantages, for example."

Caroline nodded in agreement and completed Roger's train of thought. "So the difference between the quantities ordered by the stores and the quantity I'm buying is stored in the regional warehouses."

"Which is the current situation," Roger summarized triumphantly.

"Makes sense," Paul commented, "But how does it relate to our topic?"

"Don't you see?" Roger was genuinely surprised.

"We have regional warehouses, but we continue to think and act as if we don't. Supplying to the store is not done directly from the vendor. The supply time to the store is just the time it takes to bring it from the warehouse. The supply time to the warehouse is long, as has been said. It includes production time and the long transportation by sea. But the supply time from a regional warehouse to the shop is no more than a few days; in most cases, just one day. Now go back to your sawtooth graph and see what happens when you acknowledge that the supply time is only one day. Couple it with what you said about how order lead time should be less than a day, and what do you get?"

"We get our solution!" Paul was delighted. "In spite of all the variability, we shouldn't have to hold more than two weeks or so in the shop to avoid shortages. Roger, you are something. Now it's so obvious."

"Hold your horses." Caroline did not join the celebration. "Haven't you just switched the problem from the store to the warehouse? You still have very long supply lead times and you still have all the variability."

"Not exactly," Roger said in a pleasant tone. "First of all, if they will allow me to hold the inventory rather than pushing it into the stores, we should be in a much better situation. Right now I could show you numerous cases where one store has a shortage of an SKU, while another store within the region has much too much of that same item. If we implement our method, both shops would have enough."

Still remembering some basic things from his statistics course in college, Paul realized the reason for the improvement. The variability in the warehouse, since it services many shops, is much smaller than the variability of each individual shop. Knowing that he had to think about this further, he didn't interrupt Roger, who continued to talk to Caroline.

"Secondly, the supply lead time to the regional warehouse is not necessarily long. Due to the nagging by this hunk of meat," Roger pointed to Paul, "I was forced to use a great alternative. When I'm about to run out of an SKU, I call the other warehouses. The time to get merchandise from them is usually no more than a week."

Paul picked up the graph and a pen. "Acknowledging that the regional warehouse does exist," he winked at Roger, "the sawtooth becomes more similar to this." Paul drew another pattern that oscillated much more frequently near, yet never reaching, the zero line.

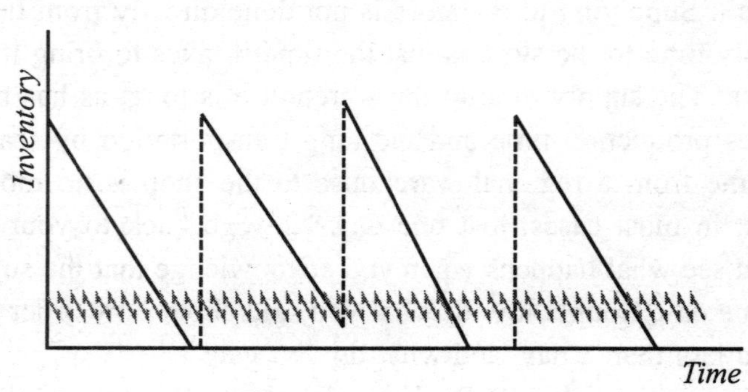

Satisfied, the three looked at each other.

"Okay, now are we ready to put together the presentation?" Roger asked Caroline.

"Almost," she answered. "I think that what we've discussed so far will be sufficient to bring the store managers to a point where they will be willing to start listening to what you have to suggest."

"Just start to listen?" Paul's voice indicated that he had been much more optimistic.

"It's a major step forward," Caroline argued. "And then the 'yes, buts' will start."

"Store managers," Roger sighed. "Very small yeses and many big buts."

"It's a major step forward from an attitude of 'it doesn't make sense, I don't want to listen'," she countered. "Guys, to be really prepared you have to do a lot more work. You have to speculate what their 'buts' will be and have a good answer for each one of those reservations."

"I am too familiar with some of those 'buts'," Paul said.

They continued to work until the small hours of the morning.

* * *

An hour had passed and so far the presentation was going well. The store managers had gathered in one of the smaller conference rooms of Hannah's Shop headquarters. Roger and Paul had finished the first stage of the presentation, and had opened the floor for questions. So far so good, Paul thought, they had succeeded in avoiding confrontation, and the hostility, which was tangible when the meeting began, had been replaced with mild curiosity.

The first question came from Carter, the youngest of the store managers."Despite all that you've said," she declared, "I still don't like the idea of shipping my entire inventory to the warehouse. If I do so, and another store is selling my items faster than I do—especially one of the bigger stores—the stock currently allotted to me will be eaten up by the time I need it. I would much prefer being in control to losing my merchandise. Losing sales means losing sales."

"Fair enough," Paul replied. "But let me ask, do you have shortages right now?"

"Far too many."

"Well, out of the shortages your store has right now, which you know you could be selling if only you had them in stock, how many of these SKUs can be found, even as we speak, idly sitting in other stores within the region?"

"I don't know," was the honest reply. "Lots, I suppose."

"Well, we checked." Paul clicked to a slide that featured a pie chart. "At the moment, our stores suffer from roughly thirty percent in shortages. This is characteristic of the industry. The finding that was amazing for us is that, right now, for sixty-eight percent of SKUs that are missing in at least one store, there is in the region, in the other stores, more than two months of inventory. Do you realize what this means?" he asked, and without waiting for an answer, continued. "It means that when we aggregate our stock in the warehouse, each store will witness an immediate drop of about two-thirds of its shortages; shortages will drop to a mere ten percent. Bottom line, this means an immediate increase of at least twenty percent in sales. Carter, don't you want your shortages to drop to only ten percent?"

"I would, but Paul, what will happen *after* two months?" Carter persisted. "Take an SKU that I do have inventory for, and another store does not. If I return my inventory to the warehouse, I accept that I am still protected for two months, because the region has, in total, two months' inventory. But what will happen after those two months? Purchasing resupplies in intervals of four to six months. I would rather hold onto my stock."

Roger, seeing that Paul was slightly irritated at this response, intervened. "Let me answer this one," he said. "This is where I step in. Today, when one store is out of an SKU, frankly I don't even blink. I know that most likely there is plenty of stock in the other shops. When you guys don't bother to manage it properly among yourselves, then it doesn't seem to be important enough to initiate a cross-shipment from another region. With so much of what one store needs sitting on another's shelves, I consider it a useless headache. But if we aggregate the stock, what will be missing from one store will be missing from all stores. Rest assured I will go out of my way to obtain those items from other regions. And there is plenty of stock in the other nine regions."

"And how successful will you be?" she asked. "If it's a fast runner for us, it is likely that it also sells well in the other regions."

"Here I can answer from experience," Roger said with assurance. "For the past few months, I've been cross-shipping more and more items, in response to the real need expressed in the Boca store. Three times out of four I don't have a problem obtaining what was needed. What it means is that you should expect your shortages to drop from thirty percent to a maximum of ten."

Dwight, sitting next to Carter, whispered something in her ear. Smiling, she replied, "If you succeed in bringing my shortages down to even half of what they are today, I'll be very pleased."

Yesterday they had been hesitant to follow Caroline's advice, to wait and not present any numbers when they first covered the resulting drop in shortages. She had claimed that they would get much more of a result if they waited until the audience drew it out through their reservations. Paul scanned the audience, trying to assess where they stood. One scowl stood out: Delacruz. Well, he figured, you can't win 'em all. Paul sipped from his glass of water before asking, "Anyone else?"

Moti, the manager of the store in Jupiter, raised his pencil and asked, "May I?"

Paul nodded.

"What if the warehouse has a problem?" the Israeli shop manager asked. "For instance, what if a truck breaks down? It happened two weeks ago—just ask Rog."

"Moti," Paul reasoned, "we're not asking you to hold only one or two days' worth of stock in the store. More like two weeks' worth. We are aware that a *force majeure*, such as a truck breaking down, can affect the equation. Even without such events, we took into account the fact that sales fluctuate. The level of variability is high, we know, but two weeks' worth of inventory should provide enough protection. Imagine having two weeks of each and every one of your SKUs. So the truck doesn't come on Tuesday, it comes on Wednesday. You don't have to hold your breath, because you just keep on selling—and selling better than before."

"I see how two weeks' worth is enough, compared to the amount we sell," Nick Nguyen, the manager of the Palm Beach branch, said.

"I'm happy you agree, Nick."

"Just a sec, I still have a problem. With only two weeks' merchandise on the shelves, won't the store be half empty?"

"So fill it with other SKUs," Paul replied. "I did it myself. I had about two thousand SKUs, and just last month I added five hundred more. The warehouse offers more than twice the amount of SKUs any store features. And the revenue from these additional items is enormous. Check the numbers; it's the reason for the last jump my store had in profitability."

Nick leaned back in his chair, obviously comfortable with the answer. Even Moti, who always looked like he smelled a fish, was sporting a small smile.

"If I may?" Eleanora was the most veteran of the managers. Paul knew that convincing her would be significant in persuading the rest.

Cleaning her glasses, she asked, "And what if it doesn't work out? What if we've handed over our inventory to the regional warehouse, signed it off on the books, and my store's performance goes nowhere, or even deteriorates?"

"Do you mean that it would work for all the other stores and just yours would be floundering?" asked Martin, the regional manager, who had been a silent partner until that moment.

"No, of course not," the manager of the Orlando branch said. "That makes no sense. I meant, what happens if this whole experiment is a failure."

"If the performance of the stores declines, we will simply ship back your original inventory," Martin answered. "This is just an internal arrangement of inventory, after all. We have a fail-safe undo button."

Two or three heads nodded, accepting Martin's words.

Delacruz emitted a short snicker.

"This is all well and good," the sleek manager of the downtown Miami store said. "But there's one small thing that bothers me. Something trivial."

"Every question is important," Paul replied, hiding his real thoughts.

"We're talking about relying heavily on the warehouse," Delacruz commented, practically sneering. "To date, none of us have been happy with the rate at which we've been replenished, and that was when they were sending whole prepackaged cartons. Your system requires the logistics staff to handle the smallest of amounts, even one measly hand towel, if that's what was sold. Are you sure that the warehouse can handle it? It doesn't just mean much more frequent deliveries, it means much more work per delivery. I'm asking because, when the warehouse crashes and burns under this impossible task, we don't want to go down with it."

Paul noticed how all the store managers tensed at this question.

"This is your field, Rog," he smiled.

"And onto slide number seventeen," Roger said, full of confidence. "It is a matter of logistics, but it's a lot easier than one would think." He went on to present the idea of the mini-warehouse in less than five minutes, utilizing three slides. "To summarize, that's the way I have been supplying Paul's store. It should answer the complete needs of this method, and it is no problem to service all of you. The only limitation

I have is the speed at which stores can join the initiative. Since I will have to arrange for the intake of all the months of inventory each store currently holds, the warehouse can only bring on board two additional shops a week."

Paul looked around at the faces of the nine store managers. Except for the grim look on Delacruz's face, everyone seemed relaxed.

Encouraged, with his best shopkeeper's smile on his face, he said, "Thanks for that question, Delacruz. Anyone else?"

Seeing no hands go up, Paul gambled.

"So, who would like to go first?" he asked, and four hands went up. Martin chose Eleanora, the most veteran store manager, and Dwight, whose store in Homestead had been at the bottom of the region's list for years.

As Martin started to thank everyone for coming, Gary interrupted, "Wait a minute, wait a minute."

Paul braced himself, expecting criticism from the man who had rejected the system just a week before.

"Paul, can you give this same presentation to my department managers?"

Chapter 19

"Can you tell a plié from a relevé?" Paul jibed.

"Not a chance," Roger answered. "I just watch Liz, and try to applaud the second she does."

During the intermission at their daughters' ballet recital, both Paul and Roger were sent to get drinks for their wives. Roger asked the bartender for two soft drinks and said to Paul, "Did you hear that Delacruz finally folded?"

"You mean that after all the faces he made during the presentation, he finally joined the rest of the region?" Paul asked. "Well, considering that last month he hit ninth place, and this month tenth, he probably ran to Martin and found an excuse to be let in."

"Oh," Roger said. "That explains it."

"So now that he's joined, your work must be easier," Paul reasoned. "Everyone's on board, you're no longer running the two distribution methods simultaneously. The system's running smoothly, right?"

"Smoothly?" Roger grimaced. "I wouldn't say smoothly."

"Why not? Didn't Martin supply the extra forklifts and manpower he promised?"

"He did," Roger calmed his friend as they started to weave their way through the crowd, back to their spouses. "And with the new arrangements, the warehouse runs fine. However, I have bigger and bigger problems with the cross-shipments. We are selling so much more that the warehouse is suffering from more and more shortages."

"But everybody transferred their stock to you. You must have more merchandise in your warehouse than ever before."

"That's true."

"More merchandise *and* more shortages? Shouldn't the former reduce the latter?" asked Paul.

"In total, we have fewer shortages than we had before we aggregated the stock in my warehouse," Roger explained. "As we predicted, there are no more cases where one shop has a shortage and I don't have the inventory to resupply it, while there is a mountain in another shop. However, the aggregation doesn't help me when there's a shortage in the entire region."

Paul placed his hand on Roger's shoulder, stopping him from stepping into a family photograph that was being taken.

"Thanks for that," Roger continued after the flash went off. "The problem is that when I announced that I would obtain fast runners from the other warehouses, I didn't realize what I was getting myself into. It's a heck of a lot of work."

"It must be," Paul said sympathetically.

"You don't understand," Roger said in frustration. "Getting cross-shipments for only your store gave me the wrong impression as to the amount of work entailed in doing it for the whole region. I went into this ditch blindfolded."

"I agree that I don't understand," Paul commented. "What are you talking about?"

Releasing a big sigh, Roger started to elaborate. "When you ran out of an SKU, it took one or two phone calls and I could put my hands on an economical batch quantity, a full six months for your shop. Of course it lasted until the next shipment from the vendor arrived. One call and I didn't have to deal with that SKU for the foreseeable future. But now I'm replenishing ten stores. The same economical batch only lasts ten days. It's not off the list; I have to deal with the same SKUs again and again. And you know how many of them I have to chase? Over a thousand."

"Is it really that bad?" Paul spotted their wives at the far end of the foyer.

"No, it's worse," Roger asserted. "It used to be that I would call two, maybe three warehouses and find what I needed. Now, after three or four rounds, quite often there's no more to be found in any of the other regions. I'm on the phone all day."

"And I bet the other warehouses aren't always happy to help out," Paul added. "I know what it was like before, when I tried to get items I needed from other stores within the region and they took my request as a sign that the item was moving well. I can only guess that as our success grows, this will only be exacerbated."

"Yes," Roger replied. "They're getting smarter by the day. Karl from Louisiana even told me straight up that he already noticed that if I'm asking him for an item, then his stores will be asking him for the same item within a month or two. The chase for the high runners seems never-ending, and more and more often it turns out to be a wild goose chase."

Paul hadn't realized how frustrating the work would be. "Are you sorry you jumped on board?" he asked.

"Not at all," Roger answered. "Sorry if I gave you the impression that I'm complaining."

"How could I get such an impression?" Paul teased him.

"Paul, its hard work but it's worthwhile. Every batch that I succeed in bringing in, I know has a direct impact on the company's profitability. A real impact. Overall, it's miles better than it used to be."

"What's miles better?" Liz asked her husband.

"Nikki's dancing." Roger kissed his wife on the cheek. "But we were talking business."

"What this time?" Caroline inquired.

"We were discussing the problems Roger has been facing," Paul said, handing his wife a paper cup. "He's been looking high and low for items that the region has been running out of. Maybe somebody from purchasing could provide us with high runners faster than usual…"

"Guys, it's not up to me," Caroline explained. "Can you give me an accurate forecast what your store will sell six months from now?"

"Last time we checked, the crystal ball hadn't arrived," Roger chuckled.

"We do the best with what we have," she summarized in her managerial tone. "As you know, it's not an in-house logistical problem, like yours was. Without an accurate forecast, I'm entirely dependent on the manufacturers."

"We're not talking about all our items," Paul pleaded. "It's about *the* items, the high runners. The region is losing a lot of money due to their shortages. My sales alone dropped by some five percent. Multiply my loss by ten stores and by the time it will take until the shipment arrives. It's mind boggling."

"I know, and the damage to the chain is ten times *that*," Caroline noted. "But, as I said, there's nothing I can do."

Roger intervened. "I think small, just my region. Is there a way for the manufacturers to bump up the small batches our region needs, move it in between the huge batches the vendors are producing for the chain?"

"I'll look into it." Caroline was noncommittal. Darren had been right all along, she thought. Half the power of the method relied on one resource—the surplus in other regions—and it was a limited resource at that. The key to resolving it, if there was one, must be in purchasing. Everyone always laid the blame on purchasing. Now she started to contemplate if they might be right.

"There's the bell," Liz said. "Let's go back in."

Chapter 20

Martin was in a good enough mood to whistle on the elevator ride to the top floor. The latest monthly report placed his region in first place again, well ahead of the others. Such a significant sales increase paired with inventory turns in the double digits wasn't just unheard of, it was practically incredible. Additionally, each store was also holding more and more SKUs. He was confident that first place would be his for quite some time.

The short yet stately regional manager walked down the corridor to the chief operating officer's office, where the secretary gestured him in. Sitting behind his dark pine desk, Christopher acknowledged his subordinate's entry and asked him to sit down.

"Congratulations on the ranking," the COO said. "I see that you've inspired your teams, and the results have been quite extraordinary. Keep up the good work."

Martin had a distinct feeling of déjà vu. "Thank you, sir. It took a lot of planning and close supervision to ensure that we would succeed as we did."

"So why did you ask to see me?" Christopher seemed curious. The regular yearly review was due to take place the following month.

"Sir, it wasn't just hard work that put my region in first place," Martin replied. "My staff has developed a new method, which now that I'm convinced is sustainable, I would like to recommend be implemented in the other regions."

"This system of yours has been working for how long—only one quarter, right?" Clearly the COO was not as enthusiastic as the regional manager. Seeing Martin nod, he continued. "Let's put this in perspective, alright? When your region's sales peaked, three months ago, I started to keep an eye on your region. I analyzed your numbers. I normalized the impact of the staggered way in which the stores embarked on this untraditional method, as well as the impact of adding new SKUs, and the true trend emerged. You got an initial jump, but every month since then your shortages grew back again and your sales decreased in proportion. According to my calculation, you'll be back where you started off in less than half a year."

"That's only because the best-selling products are snatched off the shelves," Martin said. "And it's been harder to acquire more of them from other regions."

"Exactly, but it's a trend," Christopher replied. "It was a wonderfully high peak, but as time goes by, your performance figures will return to their regular levels."

"Give it some time," Martin tried to explain. "You will see that the numbers will stay high, and that this new system can be implemented throughout the chain."

"At what expense?" Christopher's thick eyebrows moved closer together, challenging. "This onetime peak had your regional warehouse running five times as many cross-shipments as any of the other regions. Its efficiency rate dropped straight through the floor. You just said that your increase in sales is connected to the cross-shipments. What do you think will happen when the other regions realize this, and are no longer generous in what they agree to send you? Furthermore, if the whole chain works in this fashion, where would anyone get their fast runners? From the other regions, who need them as badly as yours does?"

"But even the products that aren't fast movers were selling better." Martin tried to defend his actions, but Christopher persisted.

"Not significantly enough to justify a complete revolution in the way we operate. Over the last period, your warehouse systematically held four times as much inventory as your stores, the exact opposite of the way our industry operates. Let's face it. Do you have any real supporting data to prove your method is operational and sustainable for the whole chain? No. That's why nobody else in the industry has ever done anything like this new method."

"I know that it's innovative," the regional manager said, shifting uncomfortably in his seat, "but that's not a reason not to go ahead with it. The system has many advantages. For instance, each store now holds some five hundred SKUs more than it used to, which is a major factor in the sales increase."

"Which makes it even harder to manage the logistics."

"We've solved this problem," Martin answered. "We developed a new computer system for this purpose."

No sooner had the words "computer system" left his subordinate's mouth than Christopher G. Smith's face turned into a stone wall.

"Not *another* computer system. I am at my wits' end with new computer systems. We've hardly finished sorting out the mess the last one made. I am not sure it was worth the whole ordeal. As it stands now, we've lost money on this damned software and its bugs. And the new forecasting module, it costs a fortune, it caused so many headaches, and its predictions are as ridiculous as those the old one gave. The last thing I need is for the IT people to start on *another* new project!" Christopher was more than adamant. Half rising in his seat, he towered over both his desk and Martin. "Cleaning the data, reprogramming the fields and menus, teaching all the staff again, the testing and the endless job of debugging, Henry would never agree to something like that, end of story. I am sorry about my tone, but I am not willing to approve your idea."

Christopher paused for a moment. He had no intention of disheartening his subordinate. "However," he said, sitting down again slowly, "I do realize that it has been a tremendous effort on the part of you and all the region's staff members. And you did produce excellent results... for a while. Keep up the good work."

Having been excused from his superior's office, Martin walked back down the hall, this time in a more humble mood. Clearly there would be no use in pushing his point further.

As he stepped into the elevator, he realized that it didn't really matter. He was sure that his region's success would continue. And he wasn't afraid that the other regions would stop shipping him goods. They were not doing it because of generosity. They were doing it to get rid of their huge surpluses.

He had done what he was supposed to do. He had alerted his boss to the advantages of his system. But, truth be told, if his region remained the only one that held inventory in the warehouse the way they did, and was the only one to replenish daily according to actual consumption, he would certainly retain the top position on the performance list.

And since Christopher was close to retirement, two or three years as best-performing manager would ensure that his name would be placed on the office door of the VP of operations. He could afford to be patient. The boy who had started as an assistant floor manager all those years ago, had worked his way up to southern Florida regional manager, now saw his path leading straight to the top of the mountain.

Chapter 21

Caroline was on top of her game. Two hours into the meeting with Hannah's Shop's largest supplier, she knew that she had squeezed quite a lot out of its chief executive officer. Sitting in his office in New Delhi, Caroline smiled as she signed her initials at the bottom of the order form for the next six months.

"Always a pleasure doing business," Mr. Gupta said in a proper British accent. "I look forward to hosting you again."

"Actually, there is one more thing," Caroline replied.

Just a few weeks ago she had promised Paul she would see if anything could be done to expedite SKUs that Roger could not obtain from any other warehouse. Without much hope she continued, "Last time we met, I ordered five thousand ETL sheet sets. I know they should be shipped out only three months from now, but I was wondering if you could expedite them sooner."

"How much sooner?"

"Next week would be nice," Caroline attempted. "Could you bump it up somehow?

"Why does everything have to be at the last moment?" Mr. Gupta asked, an icy glaze frosting his tone. "You know we would do almost anything we could to help you out, but this is not possible."

Caroline didn't blink an eye; she had expected this kind of a response.

The suave businessman brushed an invisible speck of dust from his lapel and continued, "If you were asking for a few hundred units, maybe, but thousands, impossible!"

"Wait," she said, surprised, "expediting a few hundred for me by next week is feasible?"

"Maybe." The Indian vendor pulled at his small moustache. "It all depends on whether the dyeing has been completed on enough fabric. How many sheet sets do you need me to expedite for you?"

Caroline ran the numbers quickly in her head. Five thousand were supposed to suffice for half a year. That meant that the chain sold some two hundred units a week. "I need two hundred," she answered. That should be enough for the South Florida region.

Seeing that Gupta had just nodded and reached for the phone, she decided to press her luck. "Two hundred a week, for each week until the bulk shipment is made." Two hundred would answer the needs of Paul's region. Two hundred every week would solve the needs of all the regions.

Mr. Gupta placed a call to his materials manager and asked him something in Tamil. While waiting for his answer he explained, "Sewing is done in small batches, a dozen dozens at most. Weaving and dyeing the fabric is a different ball game altogether. Here, to make even a small profit we must have large quantities."

Sounds erupted from the phone. He listened and said, "You are in luck. Apparently, enough for one thousand units was dyed last week. Sending you two hundred units a week would give us enough time to dye the rest of the needed fabric. Is that your desire?"

"Absolutely," Caroline said decisively.

"What about payment terms?" asked Mr. Gupta.

"Standard operating procedure." Caroline wondered why he had asked. After all, Hannah's Shop had never deviated from this rule. "Within forty-five days of the receipt of goods."

"This is unfair," Gupta complained. "You are the one who asked for partial shipment, why should I wait for my money? I understand that you delay payment until the entire order is delivered when I missed something, but in this case, you are asking for early partial delivery."

"Sorry, perhaps I should rephrase my answer," she apologized. "I should have been clearer. Within forty-five days of the receipt of every weekly shipment."

Gupta was not appeased. "Since we'll be delivering the order in multiple shipments, it will mean paying several times on the same purchase order. Can you arrange that your accounting department will not use this as an excuse to delay payment?"

Caroline had no problem guaranteeing that she would take care of it personally, realizing that payment per weekly shipment opened the door for such arrangements in the future. Now, by expediting these small quantities he wasn't doing her a favor; rather, this was a good business arrangement for both sides. She gets the merchandise she needs earlier, and he gets weekly payments for three months, instead of a bulk sum at the end of that period. That meant that his cash flow would be much smoother. No wonder he was willing to go the extra mile.

To ensure no misunderstandings, Mr. Gupta said, "You do realize that you will have to pay about three times as much for each shipment, since the amount you ordered comes nowhere near filling a container."

Caroline's face darkened. She had been seeking to increase sales for the company, not increase expenses. True, the additional sales that would result from having this fast runner available easily compensated for the extra costs of shipment, but paying more went against her upbringing.

Seeing her face, and afraid of losing what could be an advantageous arrangement, Mr. Gupta suggested, "Perhaps you have more items that we could deliver weekly until the bulk shipment? If you split enough orders into similar small quantities, it would fill a container."

Caroline smiled. She clicked open the list Roger had compiled of items he could not obtain from the other regions. In less than fifteen seconds she extracted the items purchased from Gupta's company. Turning her laptop around to face Mr. Gupta, she said, "I have about twenty more items. Is the fabric dyed for these?"

As it turned out, enough fabric was ready for only four.

"That's not enough," he said, concerned. "But wait. I see a pattern here. All the bed sets you're asking me to expedite are king-size sets. You also placed orders for queen-size. We are using the exact same fabric for both products. Maybe..."

He didn't complete his sentence, but what he had said was enough for Caroline. "If I swap, dollar for dollar, the queen-size for king-size, then your order book will be intact. Will you then agree to do the necessary diversions?"

"As long as we haven't cut the fabric, there should be no problem," Gupta assured her.

The commonality of dyed fabric and more so of raw fabric, and the willingness of both Caroline and Gupta to divert material from one product to another, helped. Almost half of the items from Roger's list that this firm provided would start to be shipped the following week.

Caroline realized that this was not the full solution, far from it. But it was a step forward, a major step. It was possible to react much faster to shortages. It was also possible to considerably shorten the production lead time for these cases.

As they closed the deal, Caroline could not help noticing something no less important. She noticed how pleased her counterpart was. He got an improved cash flow, and smaller, easier to handle quantities. It was not often that when she closed a deal she felt that both sides had come out on top. But would other vendors be as accomodating?

Chapter 22

"What do you see here?" Henry slid the monthly report across his wide desk. "I was right, Paul's performance held up much better than you predicted."

"I already saw the numbers," Christopher replied as he took a seat opposite his old friend and boss. "Both from Paul's store and the entire South Florida region. They are good. My problem is that they are too good. I don't understand it."

"Read my lips," Henry retorted. "When you reduce shortages and at the same time add more SKUs, profit does go up."

"That much I understand." Christopher's irritation showed. "But you are the one who always insists that we obey rule number whatever of yours: if we don't understand we don't move until we understand."

"What don't you understand?" Henry inquired. And in a softer voice he added, "Christopher, what is troubling you?"

"Another one of your rules," Christopher answered. "If you do not deal directly with the core problem, don't expect significant improvements. The core problem, as we've discussed it hundreds of times, is that we can't forecast accurately enough the future demand, and our supply time is very long. So we end up purchasing too few of some items and too many of others. The South Florida region's changes have nothing to do with what we purchase. The mismatch between what we buy and what we sell, remains. And as long as it remains, how can you expect a new level of performance?"

"You are right that this new way does not correct the inherent mismatch we suffer from in purchasing," Henry replied. "But it does solve the inherent mismatch we have in logistics. You are ignoring the fact that our forecast per store is even worse than the forecast that guides purchasing. We can't fix the external mismatch, but they fixed the internal mismatch; that's where this magnificent performance comes from."

He waved his hand to fend off Christopher's response. "Hear me out. Not having a good forecast on the store level caused us to ship too much to one store and not enough to another. That's what they have fixed. Utilizing the fact that internally the supply time is very short, they made the stores hold just what they need in the near future. The result is that items that used to be stuck in Boynton's store are now available for sale in the Keys. This way of utilizing the stock more intelligently is systematic. That's one thing they've done. And the other thing, which we already mentioned, is that it enables holding many more SKUs per store, also a much more prudent way of utilizing what we have."

Christopher thought about it for a while. He stared out the fourteenth-story window at the view provided by mid-town Miami.

"But no one has ever worked this way," he said, still cautious. "We'll have to move very carefully."

"Alright, mother hen. I agree to moving prudently," Henry grinned. "But I think that we've seen enough to start the ball rolling. Agreed?"

"Agreed, but we definitely have to check it further," was Christopher's answer. "I'll take care of it."

"Who do you think is the best person to head this initiative?"

"Is there any question?" Christopher looked the president of Hannah's Shop in the eye. "It's Paul's idea, it's Paul's initiative. He is the one who understands it the best. He also knows the pitfalls. Moreover, he is one of the most practical and careful managers I know. For a long time now I've asked you to stop this nonsense of wasting his time on low-level jobs. I know he wants no special treatment, but we should have kicked his *tuchus* up to the executive level a long time ago."

"Alright, I'll have a word with him," Henry was practically beaming. "What should his title be? Executive vice president for reorganization?"

"How about something simpler, something along the lines of chief operations officer?"

"What?"

"I've been here a long time, Henry," Christopher replied, running his hand through his hair, trying to pin the white strands down. "Longer than you have, actually. When you went off and had fun in college, I was the one who slaved in the store alongside your mother, God bless her soul. What did you think I would do—watch you prance off to play with the grandkids, and just sit here, waiting to receive orders from the girl I used to bounce on my knee? You've got to be kidding me. I think I've earned the right to choose my successor, having spent more than forty years here."

"My dear friend," Henry answered simply while picking up the phone, "you certainly have. Let me make a call."

"Henry! What a surprise!" Lydia exclaimed. "And to what do I owe the pleasure of hearing from you so early in the day?"

Henry smiled at his wife's humor. "What do you say we invite Paul and the kids for supper tonight. It's been too long since I last saw Ben and Lisa."

"What do I say?" Henry could practically see the expression of wonder on the other side of the phone. "What are you up to, exactly?"

"Oh, nothing, dear," he said.

"Never mind, it's probably business. I don't want to know." Lydia was clearly not buying her husband's story. "I'll ask Paul to be here at six-thirty. The kids deserve a good meal, even when their mother is overseas."

Chapter 23

Ben and Lisa ran into the Aaronson estate ahead of their father. Paul stepped through the entrance hall and into the spacious living room, where his children were embracing their grandparents. Lydia greeted him with a small embrace, a kiss on the cheek, and a quiet "they're up to something" in his ear.

Henry walked over, shook his son-in-law's hand firmly and said, "How are you, Paul? Disappointed with last night's loss to the Knicks?"

"I'm fine, thanks," Paul uttered awkwardly while wondering what Lydia meant by "they".

"Good, good," Henry boomed. "Can I get you something to drink? I've got a new bottle of scotch in my study. Why don't we go try it?"

Henry shut the sliding doors to his study. The walls had been recently painted a light shade of ecru, and the large pine desk had been replaced with an extravagant living room setting. One of the huge leather couches was occupied by Christopher.

So this is it, Paul thought, greeted Christopher, and muttered a semblance of a compliment about the new design.

"Lydia said that if I'm serious about retiring," Henry said, pouring three glasses of scotch, "then I can't have a room that looks like an executive office. Drink up, drink up!"

As Paul sank into the other couch, Henry charged on.

"We've been watching your store's progress," Henry said. "Very impressive. You've clearly been thinking outside the box."

"Thank you," Paul answered. "But I didn't have a real choice. I was merely responding to crisis. Apparently, the crisis situation forced me to operate in a better manner."

"Don't sell yourself short," Christopher said. "We've had many crises over the years. But we always went back to standard operations once it blew over."

"I almost did that as well; I was lucky that Caroline stopped me."

"We were also impressed with the speed with which you caused the entire South Florida region to adopt your way." Henry sipped from his glass and asked, "So tell me, this system you've concocted, can it be implemented across the entire chain?"

"Yes, to some extent," Paul answered with reservation. Although he had expected the ball to land in his court, he did not have a clear-cut answer. "I believe that a major part of it can be implemented across the chain successfully, and that much can be gained by it. Each region, on its own, can work this way and improve store performance."

"And yet, you are hesitant," said Henry.

"I am hesitant because a significant amount of the merchandise that is being sold in my region today is obtained via cross-shipments from the other regions," Paul explained. "Currently, we cross-ship significant amounts between regions. But when all regions are using the new method I'm afraid that a lot more cross-shipping between regions will be needed. My problem is that many of these cross-shipments will be for nothing. There is no point in transferring an SKU from one warehouse just to find two months later that the transfer created a shortage."

"And if we forbid cross-shipments all together," Christopher asked, "we'll still gain a lot, correct?"

"Then we miss an opportunity." Henry didn't like it. "So many times there are real surpluses in one region of things that are missing in another."

"Better three birds in the hand than four in the bush," was Christopher's response.

Henry turned to Paul. "What do you think?"

"I would tend to agree with Christopher, except that without cross-shipments, convincing the store managers to cooperate will be doubly hard," he said. "Only when they were promised that shortages would drop, due to more merchandise brought in from other regions, did I really get through to the store managers in my region. And without the store managers' honest cooperation, such a large change in the way they operate will take forever."

The two elderly men exchanged looks, apparently pleased to see that the young man was prudent.

"Let's take it one step back, shall we?" Henry proposed. "Among the stores in the South Florida region, there are currently no cross-shipments. Maybe we should analyze how you achieved that miracle, and see what's relevant for cross-shipments between regions."

"Alright," Paul conceded. "Although, to be honest, I am not sure any of it is relevant. A justified cross-shipment means moving surplus from one point to a point that has a shortage. At the store level, that means that any successful cross-shipment is a clear indication that there was a mistake, that too much was transferred to the store to start with; otherwise the store wouldn't have a surplus. In the new configuration, we acknowledge the very short replenishment time between the regional warehouse and the stores, and therefore we are not pushing the merchandise into the stores. We don't build the surplus so we don't need to correct by cross-shipments."

"And why do you think this isn't relevant?" Christopher asked.

"Two reasons," Paul replied. "Firstly, the much longer period of time it takes to replenish the warehouses. And secondly, warehouses aren't shipped stocks too early—they're the starting point for distribution."

A silence fell on the room, and a small smile slowly crept across Henry's face.

"According to your argument," Henry reasoned, "since we have so many cross-shipments between warehouses, that means a significant amount of our goods are in the wrong location. We've unnecessarily pushed merchandise into the warehouses, instead of supplying them with just what they require."

"We can't supply our warehouses with just what they need right away," Christopher argued. "That would leave the entire inventory of the chain sitting on the docks in Fort Lauderdale."

"Precisely," Henry agreed. "And what we need is a central warehouse, situated right there, just off the ports. The transportation from Fort Lauderdale to any of our regional warehouses is no more than a week. That's relatively short. So, if we build a central warehouse, we could dispatch inventory to the regional warehouses based on actual consumption, ensuring that every last item, whether bathrobe or pot holder, will be in the right place at the right time."

"That would mean the end of cross-shipments," Christopher said in awe. "Henry, why hadn't we thought about this a long time ago?"

"Remember what we always said," Henry growled. "If it is embarrassingly obvious, it must be right."

Paul, who had been listening intently, suddenly realized, "Henry, with all SKUs held in one place, you won't just be taking care of the internal logistics. Half of Caroline's problem will also be solved."

Henry smiled. "We will know exactly what to deliver to which point, and when. The stores and the regional warehouse will not generate orders, they will be replenished according to their actual daily sales."

"So purchase requests will be generated only by the central warehouse." Paul was getting excited. "Inventory will actually decrease. We'll set a new ROI record."

Clapping Paul on the back, Henry said, "I like your way of thinking, son."

"Thank you, Henry."

"But this leaves us with a lot of work to do," Christopher grinned. "We have to locate a large enough warehouse in the port, configure the layout…"

"Calculate how much inventory it should hold, arrange the delivery frequency," Henry continued the point. "There are a lot of unanswered questions."

"We need an exceptional warehouse manager." Christopher rubbed his chin.

"I know just the man for the job," Paul offered. "Roger Wood, the South Florida regional warehouse manager. He's been my partner in the process. The logistic arrangements were completely his ideas; we never could have succeeded without him. And he's already a company man, with a lot of experience. Also, since he lives nearby, you won't have to pay for relocation."

"Excellent, I'll have my secretary arrange an interview," Christopher said, and leaned towards Paul. "But I think we need someone to oversee the whole solution, not just the central warehouse. Such a change impacts every store and every warehouse, not to mention an overhaul to our computer system."

"Yes, someone who knows a lot about the company." Henry stared at the ceiling, feigning innocence. "Someone whose *tuchus* needs kicking in the right direction..."

Paul blushed.

"Paul," his father-in-law said, "I appreciate the fact that you wanted to learn the ropes, from the bottom up. I know you are a very capable individual. Your sharp eye and talents have been prominent in every position you've held. My good friend here has been nudging me for the past five years that you should start visiting his office, to take over when he retires. And it's time we both started listening to him."

"I'm honored," Paul managed to say.

"Hold on one second, Henry," Christopher said, "did you just say you would finally start listening to me? I had to wait until I retired for that to happen?"

Chapter 24

It was the end of a long day's work and Henry Aaronson had straightened the remaining documents on his desk, placing a few of them in his briefcase. He stepped out into the hallway of the top floor of the Hannah's Shop headquarters. He noticed a light was still on in Caroline's office. He wondered if she was working so hard because she wanted to, or because she had to. He had placed considerable pressure on her when he had announced she would be his successor, and he hoped that she realized, as he did, that she was more than ready to do so.

He checked his watch before knocking on her door.

"It's eight-forty-eight P.M.," he said. "Burning the midnight oil?"

"Is it that late?" Caroline said. Looking up, she blinked her eyes. "I'd lost track of the time."

"What's so urgent that you couldn't go home to Paul and the kids?"

"It's the external mismatch," she said. "I can't get it out of my head, so I've been spending a lot of time on it. I have a solution for part of the issue, but there's a huge problem I can't seem to overcome."

"My girl, you are much better than I am." Henry walked in and sat down. "All I managed to do was to go around in circles."

"So you've been thinking about it, too?"

Henry grinned. "For about the last forty years." In a more sober tone he added, "But for the last three months, ever since Paul showed that the internal mismatch can be resolved, I've been consumed by trying to figure out how to extend his solution to solve the external mismatch."

"Me too," Caroline admitted. "For years I was absolutely convinced that there was nothing to be done about the mismatch between purchasing and actual consumption; that the deadly combination of inaccurate forecasts and the long replenishment time doomed us to suffer from a huge number of shortages on the one hand and from huge surpluses on the other."

"That's exactly what Christopher and I believed. No wonder it took so much time before we were convinced that Paul's solution works. So, what progress have you made?"

"I thought that the essence of Paul's solution would provide a good starting point," she explained. "So, in trying to see how it would be relevant for resolving the external mismatch, I tried to truly understand this essence; its conceptual framework."

"Very good," Henry said, pleased. "I did something similar. Let me assume that you already figured out that at the base of his approach is the realization that even though the forecast is lousy, it is not uniformly lousy across the company."

Caroline smiled. "It took me quite some time and digging into my college notes. But yes, I figured it out." And then she summarized her findings. "The forecast is the worst at the store level, and we can't change that. According to chaos theory, trying to predict accurately what the demand will be for a particular SKU in a particular store is as useful as trying to accurately predict the weather a month in advance."

After spending considerable sums of money in vain on computerized forecasting systems, Henry had invested his time in studying the field in depth, just to reach the same gloomy conclusion. He took over. "But the demand from a regional warehouse is the aggregated demand of all the stores it services. This aggregation causes the forecast at the regional level to be about three times more accurate than the forecast of each store. This is fundamental statistics. And the forecast at the central warehouse level, which aggregates the demand from all ten regions, is three times better again."

"Correct," Caroline agreed. "And Paul's solution is based on taking advantage of the better forecast that already exists. Retail chains should not hold the inventories at the worst forecast level; the one from the stores. Instead they should hold most of the inventories at the best forecast level; the one from the central warehouse. And use the flexibility provided by the relatively short replenishment time to direct the merchandise to where reality is showing it is needed."

"Nice way of putting it, my girl," Henry commented. "But this is where I got stuck, within the company boundaries. That's as far as the aggregation train took me. You said you have a solution. Have you managed to push it further? If so, I must be missing something."

Proudly, Caroline answered, "If we go beyond the company's boundaries, into the manufacturers themselves, there is no additional geographic aggregation. However, there is another type of aggregation that continues to improve the accuracy of the forecast." Seeing that her father wasn't following her, she explained, "Many different SKUs are produced from the same dyed fabric. On average, about ten different SKUs are made from the same fabric."

Slowly, Henry said, "I still don't see how this relates to our problem."

"I can relate to that; it wasn't clear at the start for me, either," she said. "We're used to thinking about the manufacturers' environment as a rigid environment: an environment where the production of large batches is determined months in advance. But my recent interactions with our large suppliers have shown me that this rigidity is not inherent for the manufacturer; it's our doing. You see, after the fabric is dyed, they don't work in large batches. And as long as we protect them by placing umbrella orders which guarantee certain dollar amounts purchased over an extended period of time, they won't have any problem adjusting their sewing schedule with just a week's notice." She paused to allow Henry to digest the ramifications.

It didn't take him long. "This means that we should hold the inventories at the most accurate forecast point; at the dyed fabric stage. And since the manufacturer has full flexibility after that stage, there is no point deciding, months and months in advance, which SKUs we'll need. We streamline the needed orders according to the actual consumption from the central warehouse. My girl, you are something."

Caroline blushed a bit at the compliment and elaborated. "We place small orders, weekly orders, just the transportation time in advance. Transportation time plus one week for cutting and sewing, to be exact. Over the last three months, we started working this way with all our large suppliers. They love it. It gives them security for the long run—I guarantee the total monthly purchases for six months into the future—and it gives them stability, in both their operation and their cash flow."

"Brilliant. But darling, your flexibility to adjust the quantities you need depends on them having enough dyed fabric. How did you make sure of that?"

"Simple," her smile radiated from rosy cheeks, "I purchase the dyed fabric three months in advance, and the manufacturers hold it on their premises."

Henry rolled it over in his mind. "I see," he said. "That is the most accurate forecast point, so the risk of purchasing too little or too much is the smallest." Seeing her grin, he continued, "You're not afraid to get stuck with surplus fabric because you can always find a use for it, and you are also making sure you won't run out of fabric. Smart girl. Very nice. So where is your problem? It seems like you've solved all the problems."

"Not quite. What I've done so far is to reduce the dependency on our long-term forecast and to cut the replenishment time in half. But to take full advantage of this, we should reduce accordingly the inventories we hold in the central warehouse."

"Of course," was Henry's immediate reaction. "We can reduce them to less than half. Haven't you started already?"

"Dad, I don't dare to."

Henry didn't rush to ask why. He realized what the reason was. "You don't trust the suppliers," he stated rather than asked.

"How can I?" Caroline released her frustration. "Of course they promise to deliver on time. And for most of them, I know that they mean it. But what happens when another client comes along and presses them to deliver early. Under such pressure they'll usually fold, and we'll end up with a late delivery. As long as we hold months and months of inventory there's no real damage, or at least it's masked by the fact that inventory is missing anyhow for so many SKUs. But, now, if we lower the inventories, the damage will be real—and very visible."

"If so," Henry acknowledged the problem, "we must make sure that it is in the interest of the supplier to deliver on time."

"How? By demanding hefty penalties? There is no way they will agree to that." Caroline dismissed the suggestion. "Especially now that I'm asking them to become our partners; asking them to change completely the traditional arrangement between textile suppliers and retailers."

"So if you can't use the stick, use the carrot."

"Give them bonuses?" Caroline asked. "For doing what they've committed to do?"

"Caroline, soon you will no longer be the EVP of purchasing. So will you please stop following the instinct of trying to squeeze every cent from the suppliers? You said the key phrase. You are asking them to become our partners. Partners also share in the benefits."

Caroline made a funny noise. "When you entered, I was busy calculating the benefits we would gain if we could fully trust our vendors and reduce the inventories. It's huge. Also, it opens new horizons. It changes the risk-reward ratio to the extent that I could really contemplate moving into fashion merchandise. I had been playing with the figures in order to increase my motivation to find a solution. But only now, due to your comment, I see that therein lays the solution. Our gains would be so large that we could easily afford to give bonuses to the good performers."

"Just tie it directly to our performance," Henry cautioned her.

"I'll tie it to them helping us to improve our performance," she reasoned. "Their bonus should be in proportion to our inventory turns on their products." Seeing no response from her father, she added, "And, of course, to be entitled to the bonus, their due date performance can't drop below ninety-five percent for the previous three months. This way they are bound to resist any pressure from a competitor to give them higher priority."

It didn't take Henry more than a few seconds to pass judgment. Instead of saying anything, he got up, walked over to his daughter, and kissed her on the forehead.

"Now that you've found a solution I sought for forty years, like Moses in the desert," Henry smiled warmly, "do you still have doubts that you are suited to sit in my chair?"

Chapter 25

The four grandchildren sang Chanukah songs together. Henry and Lydia couldn't have felt prouder. Ryan and Sean, Darren's twins, had lovely singing voices, as did their fair-haired cousin Lisa. And no one was surprised that Ben, whose voice was changing, sang in the quietest voice possible.

After the performance received a well-deserved ovation, Paul and Caroline brought out the *dreidels* and gold-wrapped chocolate coins. As the Aaronson clan sat down to start gambling, Henry touched Darren on the shoulder.

"Mind joining me in the study?"

Darren settled into the leather sofa, poised for battle. Every time his father got him alone, he thought, it was the same old story. The old man would say how wrong he was to have left Hannah's Shop. This time, with the new spectacular numbers, his gloating would be unbearable. Darren vowed to try and control his temper.

Henry sat down opposite Darren and asked, "What's your assessment of the future of the company, son?"

At least the tone in which the question was asked was pleasant, Darren thought, carefully choosing his words. "I think that the company was solid to start off with. And what Paul and Caroline have come up with will transform Hannah's Shop into something a breed apart."

"Hmmm..." was Henry's only comment.

"Dad, over the past ten years I've gained deep knowledge on how to assess companies. Paul and Caroline helped me perform an in-depth due diligence. My professional opinion is that you don't have to be worried.

This couple will most probably face numerous difficulties in implementing their new ideas, but their ideas are solid and they have what it takes. It shouldn't take more than a year before the company's performance will set new records in home textile retail; in profitability, in inventory turns, in the number of SKUs per square feet, in cash flow…in every parameter."

Henry did not reply. He just continued to look concerned.

Not knowing what to say, Darren added, "In one year the company will have the springboard for becoming the real thing."

"Springboard," Henry repeated. "What do you mean by springboard?"

The inquisition again, Darren thought. Don't fudge, but answer his question politely. It will soon be over. Aloud he answered, "As a venture capitalist I'm trained to look for companies that have succeeded in developing a decisive competitive edge. But any competitive edge gives the company just a limited window of time; sooner or later the competition will close in. Real business smarts means capitalizing on your competitive edge while it lasts."

Henry's eyes narrowed as he asked, "And you think that Hannah's Shop has, or soon will have just such a competitive edge?"

"Without a doubt," Darren said. "I also believe that since it stems from a challenge to the most fundamental principles of the business, it will last for several years. The hardest thing for competitors to emulate is a fundamental change. It will probably take them ten years, maybe even fifteen."

"And what do you think Hannah's Shop should do in this window of time?" Henry asked.

"Capitalize on it. Expand. It took you a lifetime to bring the company from one small shop to a chain that spans the Southeast. This rare opportunity should be used to speed things up dramatically."

To Darren's surprise, Henry said, "I agree. So in ten years max, we should cover the entire country?"

Darren decided to take a risk and express his true opinion. "With such a phenomenal edge, thinking in terms of just the U.S. is missing the boat. I would say that the target should be international expansion."

A silence fell on the room. Darren waited for a strong reaction or at least a lecture in prudency from his father. Instead, Henry said, quite calmly, "No matter how profitable Hannah's Shop could be, such an expansion can't possibly be financed from internal revenues. Are you going to try and convince me to bring investors in?"

"What's the point?" Darren replied. "You'll never agree to sell even one share of the company, nor risk the company by loading it with debt."

"That's right," Henry said firmly. But then, to Darren's surprise, he continued, "Does this mean we should just forget that—what did you call it—rare opportunity, phenomenal edge?"

"That would be a grave mistake," Darren said decisively.

"So?"

He's looking for a fight, Darren thought. *Fine with me.* He said coolly, "There are other ways to raise money."

"That's what I was thinking, too," Henry said, to Darren's astonishment. "What do you think about franchising?"

Darren almost jumped to his feet. "Dad, are you serious?"

"Yes, I am. Do you know how to construct something prudent?"

Struck speechless, Darren could only nod.

Henry asked, "How much time will it take you?"

"These things take a while. At least six months."

"Good. But son, we have a bigger problem." Henry stood up and poured them each a drink. "Darren, I divide people into two camps. Those who measure themselves by how they do relative to some reference, and those who couldn't care less about what others have achieved. These individuals measure themselves according to the inherent potential of the situation they are in."

He paused to allow Darren to comment. Darren knew exactly what his father was talking about. This was the most frustrating part of his work. Many companies looked for investors, but the majority of them did not have what he was looking for. They didn't have the potential to generate high returns, or the investment in them was too risky. The problem with what he considered the real opportunities, the companies with great potential, was that they compared themselves to the norm, and as a result they were satisfied with what they were achieving. They were doing very well; they were doing much better than their competitors. And it was so difficult, sometimes impossible, to open their eyes to the fact that there is so much more; that the inherent, solid potential that they had created could be used to dwarf whatever they had already achieved.

"I understand," Darren assured his father. "And you suspect that Caroline and Paul belong to the first camp? That they will be satisfied with what they are creating now? I think that you are underestimating them."

"Really?" Henry said a bit sarcastically. "Son, imagine that you tell your sister that whatever they are going to achieve, being number one in profitability, being the benchmark of the industry, et cetera, all of it is just a—what word did you use? Just a springboard. What do you think her reaction will be?"

Darren's expression revealed that for him it was a rhetorical question.

"So you agree that there is no point pressing the issue on them now," Henry said.

"And there is no way to move them," Darren added, "before they can clearly see where the money needed for the rapid expansion will come from."

Henry smiled, "Rapid expansion? More like an explosion. Son, when the time is right…"

"We shouldn't wait for too long," Darren interjected, "From my experience I can tell you that unless they are shaken up they will start to move only when some competitors succeed in closing the gap. Then it will be too late."

"Son, when the time is right," Henry repeated, "I will not be in the position to push for it. If there is one sure way to ruin the company, it's if after I retire, I continue to be a backseat driver. Do you understand that the ball will be in your court?"

Darren emptied his glass. He took a deep breath and said, "Don't worry. I'm eager and able to convince them." With a big smile he added, "Of course, I'll also arrange for the franchisees and take my cut."

Henry stood up. "And to think that all these long years I was convinced that you'd made the wrong decision, that you just threw your life away. Come son, let's join the family. I want to make my apology to you in front of your mother."

Chapter 26

Darren walked into Caroline's office.

"Funny, I thought you would have made more changes to Dad's office," he said.

Caroline and Paul laughed. Nothing had remained the same since she had assumed the presidency a year ago.

"I come bearing gifts," Darren stated, and placed a cardboard cup carrier that held three cups of coffee, each stamped with the logo of a well-known brand. "Black for Paul, Colombian blend for Cara, and the new something-in-Italian-chino for me."

"Matthew could have made us coffee," Caroline said.

"I know," Darren replied, smirking. "But this is *good* coffee."

After trading stories about their kids, Paul said, "Alright, down to business. You asked to see us about the expansion. I prepared all the reports for you to review. As you can see, for the last year we've been expanding at twice the rate of any of our competitors. We just finished the preliminary work on our third new region." Paul was obviously proud of this achievement.

"That's great," Darren said, but did not look at the report, "but that's not why I'm here."

"What?" Caroline asked. "You specifically stated that you wanted to have a meeting with us about the expansion."

"Yes, yes," he answered. "About the expansion you *should* be doing, not about the snail's pace at which you are planning to move."

"We're moving twice as fast as the competition!" Paul lifted up the reports he had prepared. "Two new regions in one year. Where I come from, outrunning everyone else is called fast."

"You are three times as profitable and your stores turn the inventory six times as fast," Darren retorted. "But Paul, why compare yourselves to the competitors? Why not concentrate on what makes sense for us to do?"

"He has a point," Caroline said before Paul could object. "We didn't devise the way Hannah's Shop is running by looking at what the competitors were doing." Seeing that her husband agreed, she turned back to Darren and said, "Al-right, start from the top, please."

"Hannah's Shop has a considerable advantage," the venture capitalist said, "one that should be capitalized upon before the competitors start to close the gap. We can, and should, rapidly expand the geographic reach of the chain, and for that we need money. Now, before you start your assault, I agree that we should not bring in outside money, neither investors nor loans, nor should we mortgage the family's assets."

"One of Dad's rules: what you have is what you have," Caroline quoted.

"And that's what we've done so far regarding expansion," explained Paul. "I took into account only the money we'll generate, considering, of course, that as we grow we also have to increase our cash reserves. And Darren, no matter how attractive the opportunity is, neither Caroline nor I will agree to sail too close to the wind."

"I'm not suggesting you do that," Darren assured them. "But before discussing how fast we should go, do you mind spending a few minutes discussing what the money is needed for to begin with?"

"Isn't it obvious?" Caroline asked.

"Don't you see that he has an ace up his sleeve, Cara?" Paul asked. "Okay Darren, in order to expand we need money for building the infrastructure and for opening the stores."

Darren picked up the ball. "At the store level you've reduced the number one item; we need just a fraction of the conventional investment in inventory. You also reduced drastically the investment needed for the inventory held at the regional warehouse."

"Darren," Paul started to lose his patience, "a large chunk of the money goes to advertising. And don't fool yourself; the fact that we are a brand name in one area is far from being enough when we expand, even to an adjacent state. This year alone I laid out exorbitant sums building our brand name in just two new states."

"Exactly," Darren smiled, and suggested, "But perhaps there's a different way of building your brand name."

"Like what?" Paul asked, and took a sip from the coffee his college roommate had brought.

"I had a revelation," Darren reported. "You open many stores at once within a small area, and *presto,* you have a brand name without spending a dime on advertising. It's brilliant!"

"So, your so-called brilliant idea is that we should save money on advertising by laying out a small fortune all at once?" Caroline asked.

"And who says it can be done at all?" Paul asked. "Suppose we open all these stores, and because we don't have enough publicity, they all fall flat?"

"You want proof that it works?" Darren queried, a smile on his face. "Take a look at what's in your hands."

"Some java?" Caroline asked.

"Yes, Cara," Paul said, understanding his brother-in-law's idea. "Look at the logo on the cups. Remember how this coffee company opened its stores—seven in midtown Miami in one night, without any ads at all? They practically ran the competition out of town."

"Alright, I'm nibbling, but not fully biting just yet," Caroline said. "But to get back to my earlier question, where will we find that much money to open that many stores so rapidly? Knowing you, Darren, I'd guess that you want us to open in ten or even twenty regions a year, at least."

"Who says you need money?" Darren replied.

"You open a store, you rent a location," Paul stated.

"You renovate it. You hire staff. You invest in the merchandise. There is a lot of money involved."

"I know that," Darren replied. "But who said it has to be *our* money? We could franchise the brand. That way we retain control of the chain without mortgaging any of the assets."

"But why would anyone agree to be a franchisee for Hannah's Shop?" Caroline asked.

"I don't trust a franchisee to properly run a shop. Definitely not the way we would run it," Paul added.

"Any more bullets for me to dodge?" Darren asked cynically. "We're on the same side, remember?"

Smiling, Caroline answered, "Prove it."

"Have you ever heard of mezzanine finance?" Seeing their blank look, Darren continued, "I thought so. It is a channel that many conservative yet sophisticated investors choose. These are people who are not willing to take the high risk of investing in the stock exchange or, God forbid, a start-up company. But they are looking for a much higher return than the abysmal returns you get on bonds."

"Sounds okay so far," Caroline commented.

Darren pressed on. "They don't want to spend the time and money to do proper due diligence, and they don't want to be involved in running a company. So they seek out ways to lend their money to a solid company with a demonstrated track record, at an interest rate of around twenty-five percent. They don't ask for collateral, instead their security comes from the rights to convert to an ownership or equity interest in the company if the loan is not paid back in time and in full."

"Are you joking?" Caroline asked sharply. "We don't want a loan, and we are certainly not willing, under any circumstances, to give equity in the company."

"Sis, will you trust me for a second? I don't have any intention of doing straight mezzanine finance. I just want you to understand the frame of mind of this type of investor; what they are actually looking for."

"Carry on," Paul said, "I think I see where you're going with this."

"Sorry Darren," Caroline apologized. "You just caught me by surprise. I'm with you, please continue."

Darren smiled, took his time to finish his coffee, and only then continued. "Do you know the incremental return on investment for one single store in a home-textile retail chain?"

"No," Caroline answered. "We know the ROI for a chain, not for a single store, but we can do a rough estimate. A good home-textile retailer does about six percent profit on sales, and turns the inventory in a store about three times a year. Considering all the usual factors, the ROI of a single store should be around fifteen percent."

"That would be my guess as well," Darren commented. "And what do you think is the incremental ROI of a single Hannah's Shop store?"

"I knew it," Paul said with a wide smile. "I knew you were leading us to this point. Our investment in a shop is about half the norm and our profits are about three times higher. Our ROI is definitely above one hundred percent. For someone looking for a return of twenty-five percent it's almost too good to be true."

"You don't offer something that is too good to be true, not to a conservative investor," Darren said. "But if the investor's money is invested in a store of a solid company; and Hannah's Shop having been in business for over fifty years, has zero debt and an excellent reputation, is certainly solid. And there are the statistics of more than one hundred stores, each showing a return of investment of over one hundred percent a year. And the investor is the first in line, before the company takes a cent from the profits of that store. And his share will be thirty percent a year on his investment in that particular store of the Hannah's Shop chain. With all that as a background, will the investor be concerned that he won't get his thirty percent per year?"

"Just to make sure," Caroline checked, "the investor will invest in the new store, and in the unlikely event that the store's profitability is less than thirty percent on his investment, he will not have a claim on the *company*, only on the assets of that particular store."

"Precisely," her brother replied. "And Hannah's Shop has an option to buy back his investment after a few years at a predetermined price."

"That's not franchising," Paul commented.

"It is in the sense that per store you have an outside entity, and you don't invest in the store, just in the supporting infrastructure," Darren stated. "And for that, taking into account that you don't have to invest much in the regional warehouse inventory, Hannah's Shop has more than enough money to open many regions per year."

"We'll have to open clusters of shops to minimize the advertising budget," Paul recapped, "but what I like most is that operations are fully under our control."

"We'll have to run the books separately for each such shop," Caroline noted.

"Yes," Paul agreed. "But look on the bright side—I know a lot of store managers who will be glad to get equity in the store they are running."

Hearing the back-and-forth between his sister and her husband, Darren warned himself to keep his mouth shut. His work was done; they were now busy convincing themselves.

"That's important," Caroline said. "It provides us with an excellent promotion channel, especially if we expand rapidly."

"Let me tell you, for the good store managers it is a gift from heaven," Paul reported. "Knowing that seven individuals within your store are all vying for your position is not fun. Currently we have many talented department and floor managers who have nowhere to go within the company. Not only would this provide a real option for promotion for them, it would act as an incentive for other employees to work harder."

"It's probably the right way to go. Of course, there are a million and one details that have to be hammered out." Turning to Darren she added, "But before I'll even consider it, there is one issue on which I need an answer from you. We have no idea how to do this; how to find investors, how to negotiate the deals, what should and shouldn't be in the contracts. We need your help."

"Have no fear, my dear sister." Darren grinned like the Cheshire Cat. As he had told his father earlier that morning, he had all his bases covered. "I would love to provide my services. For my usual finder's fee, of course."

Epilogue

The view from the penthouse deck was breathtaking. Paul stared at the lights of São Paulo, which went on and on as far as the eye could see. Combined with the cool breeze, they made the night of the Brazilian investors' party into something almost miraculous. A light samba played, and the sounds of conversation could be heard from within.

Suddenly, Paul heard Darren's voice. "So, has Ben decided what he wants to do, now that he's completed his degree?" The New Yorker stepped out onto the terrace, champagne flute in hand.

"I have to tell you, there must be something wrong with that young man," Paul joked. "He started working in Hannah's Shop. And he's asked to move through the company slowly, learning the ropes from the bottom up."

"You must be proud," Darren noted.

Paul smiled as his wife joined them on the balcony.

"Ah, there you are: the dynamic duo," she said. "I wanted to have a word with you guys."

Just like Dad, Darren thought, *business always comes first. I guess it comes with the territory.*

"Now that everything's moving so smoothly, I wanted to raise a subject that's been bothering me for some time," she said, sitting down on a cushioned bench. "Darren, you've become quite an expert on franchising, haven't you?"

"I guess so." Her brother shrugged his shoulders, feigning modesty. "Let me see, with successful franchises working across the U.S. and

Canada, Europe, China, Australia, and now Brazil, I guess I've become a bit of a maven in the field."

"So why haven't you been as active outside Hannah's Shop?" Caroline inquired. "I mean, why haven't you used your knowledge in the field with any other business?"

Darren leaned against the railing and replied, "I've been overseeing the expansion for nine years, and only now you ask?"

"Cara has a good question," Paul said as he sat down next to his wife. "I mean, it's not like we ever stopped you from using our ideas elsewhere."

"I don't know," Darren said, obviously uncomfortable. "I never found the right opportunity."

That didn't sound right to Paul. He knew his brother-in-law better than that. "In nine years there were no opportunities?" he asked.

"I tried," the venture capitalist admitted. "But when I approached companies and revealed even a portion of the ideas you two developed, they all said that I should concentrate on investments and leave the operational side to them. The only way I could persuade top management was by buying the company. But there was no point doing that because for sure I would get stuck, since I don't know how to persuade middle management."

"I can understand your frustration," Paul stated.

"I see the potential, and how it's going to be wasted," Darren continued. "There is so much that could be done with these concepts. We could buy whole chains and within a year or two increase their value tenfold. I could put Warren Buffett to shame."

"So what you're saying is that you need an operations guy next to you, to complete the picture, right?" Caroline asked. "Like Paul."

Neither Paul nor Darren could believe what Caroline just said. Was she proposing that Paul leave the company?

"Honey," Paul asked, "what are you talking about?"

Caroline took her husband's hand in hers and said, "Paul, you are an amazing person. I love you from here to Miami and back. But you're becoming insufferable."

"What?" Paul was surprised to hear this.

"Everywhere we go, you keep finding problems," she replied. "Like the time you went shopping for that pitcher's shirt for Ben and they had run low on it, so you gave a lecture to the young man behind the counter."

"Quarterback's shirt," Paul muttered.

"Whatever," she said. "Or when we bought that eyeliner I like, and you gave that nice lady an earful on how the display has to be always complete, and that they should order things daily."

"But that's just because they could be doing better, and it's not so hard to do it," Paul argued passionately. "They don't need a crystal ball, nor should they wait for their pipes to burst. Why not make things better now?"

"See what I mean?" Caroline turned to her brother. "I can't take him anywhere anymore."

"Never mind that," Paul went on. "We work together, we make a good team."

"That doesn't mean I need to hold you back, clip your wings," Caroline said. "You get so frustrated because you see how our ideas can be implemented in other fields. Keeping you locked in home textiles would be nothing more than a selfish act. I couldn't do that to you."

Of course she was right, Paul realized. This had been his heart's desire. He appreciated Caroline all the more for bringing it up. Her act left him speechless.

Luckily, Darren spoke up. "And now that you've fired this *shegetz*, you want me to partner with him?"

"Would you let anyone else get their hands on him?" she asked. "Just think about it. Together, you could take any field—sporting goods, electronics, cosmetics, what have you—and do for it what you did for Hannah's Shop. After all, Darren, you were the one who showed us that you always have to think bigger, better, that more can be done, even when you're at the top, even if it seems almost unthinkable at the time. Now there's nothing holding you back."

Paul smiled and lifted his glass for a toast. "The sky's the limit."

"No," Darren grinned, and clinked his glass against Paul's. "Even the sky's not the limit."

Other books by : Eliyahu M.Goldratt and Jeff Cox

THE GOAL
By: Eliyahu M. Goldratt

Written in a fast-paced thriller style, The Goal is a gripping novel, which is transforming management thinking throughout the world. It is a book to recommend to your friends in industry - even to your bosses - but not to your competitors.

Alex Rogo is a harried plant manager working ever more desperately to try improve performance. His factory is rapidly heading for disaster. So is his marriage. He has ninety days to save his plant - or it will be closed by corporate HQ, with hundreds of job losses. It takes a chance meeting with a professor form student days - Jonah - to help him break out of conventional ways of thinking to see what needs to be done.

The story of Alex's fight to save his plant is more than compulsive reading. It contains a serious message for all managers in industry and explains the ideas, which underline the Theory of Constraints (TOC), developed by Eli Goldratt.

Dr. Eliyahu M.Goldratt is an internationally recognized leader in the development of new business management concepts and systems, and acts as an educator to many of the world's leading corporations. He is the originator of the Theory of Constraints (TOC) and his ideas are beginning to revolutionize the way companies work.

He obtained his Bachelor of Science degree from Tel- Aviv University and his Master of Science and Doctorate of Philosophy in Physics from Bar-llan University. In addition to his pioneering work in manufacturing management, he holds patents in other areas, ranging from medical devices to temperature sensors. Dr. Goldratt is a frequent contributor to industrial and scientific journals.

His lectures at universities of Britain, Continental Europe and the USA are sought after and very well received.

THE GOAL II : It's Not Luck -The Sequel to THE GOAL
By: Eliyahu M. Goldratt

Alex Rogo, the hero of ***The Goal***, has had a great year, having been promoted as the Executive Vice President of UniCo, a diversified conglomerate with the responsibility of managing three recently acquired companies. His team of former and new associates is in place and the future looks secure and exciting.

How Alex applies the Theory of Constraints to Sales, Marketing, Inventory Control and Business Strategy, to overcome cruel challenges and eventually emerge a winner, forms rest of the story.

As Alex grapples with problems at work and at home, we learn the full scope of Eli Goldratt's powerful Thinking Process techniques for solving problems using his (Goldratt's) Current Reality Tree, which incorporates UnDesirable Effects (UDEs), and then a Future Reality. Some excellent business wisdom is presented including techniques like Vendor Managed Inventory. The will find these techniques effective not only in business application but at a personal level as well.

CRITICAL CHAIN
By: Eliyahu M. Goldratt

CRITICAL CHAIN, a gripping fast-paced business novel, does for Project Management what Eli Goldratt's other novels have done for Production and Marketing. Dr. Goldratt's books have transformed the thinking and actions of management throughout the world.

If you have read THE GOAL and GOAL II you will want to read CRITICAL CHAIN because you understand how Eli Goldratt's books can change how you think about business.

If you have not read THE GOAL and the GOAL II, this book will introduce you to Dr. Goldratt's Thinking Processes, and you will understand why Fortune Magazine calls him "a guru to industry," and Business Week describes him as a "genius."

NECESSARY BUT NOT SUFFICIENT
TOC Business Novel for IT

By : Eliyahu M. Goldratt with Eli Schragenheim & Carol A. Ptak

After reading the newspapers and following the sharp oscillations of the stockmarket, it becomes apparent that hi-tech companies are of a different breed. Never before have the chances of making a fortune been so realistic and never before have large companies been so fragile. What is really going on inside these hi-tech companies? What types of pressures and challenges are they facing? And how do they cope?

Computer software providers, especially the ones that specialize in handling the data needs of organizations, are prime examples of these volatile companies. In the nineties we witnessed their growth from small business into multi-billion dollar giants. No wonder investors were attracted.

In 1998 it was easy for such companies to raise as much money as they wanted. But now, investments funds have dried up. Why? And more importantly, is there a way to reverse the trend? This book gives the answers.

PRODUCTION THE TOC WAY

By: Eliyahu M.Goldratt

While most readers could perceive and agree with the "common sense" of The Goal, they nevertheless had difficulty implementing the Theory of Constraints, for they could not identify the real constraint - they continued to try to improve everything they knew how to improve, they continued to justify investments based on cost calculations, they continued to make decisions based on product-cost impact. However; they continued to ignore the fundamental difference between a transfer batch and a process batch, they even continued to measure efficiencies and variances. And this was done even in companies where the President made The Goal mandatory reading!

Why?

The obstacles, identified, being:

a) Lack of ability to propagate the message throughout the company

b) Lack of ability to translate the learning into workable practices

c) Lack of ability to persuade the decision makers to allow the change of some of the measurements.

Goldratt's answers for overcoming these obstacles were in the form of a precise verbalization of the need to change the measurements and the rules of logistical procedure; Drum-Buffer-Rope and the Buffer Management principles. Once again, many managers did not get the expected benefits. So Dr.Goldratt developed a computer game. A game is probably easier to understand than a story. It is in the form of a computer simulation -where a factory -situation is simulated. He called the book Production the TOC Way.

We present the Production the TOC Way along with a work book and the computer simulation. This book is a must for all those anxious and eager to implement The Goal.

Other Books from PQP on TOC

DEMING & GOLDRATT

The Theory of Constraints and The System of Profound Knowledge

By **Domenico Lepore and Oded Cohen**

This book presents a step-by-step guide to implementing the management systems of Dr.W.Edwards Deming and Dr. Eliyahu M. Goldratt in the form-of an integrated ten-step process called: THE DECALOGUE.

The ten steps of the Decalogue stem from one fundamental concept: in order to manage effectively we must be able to predict the outcome of our decisions. Prediction is possible only within a system in a state of statistical control. Achieving such a state enhances our possibilities of getting the maximum performance from our system.

Managing a stable system effectively is possible through the effective management of its constraints. Moreover, constraints are not only internal to the system; very often what constrains our performance is our inability to sell what we are able to produce or provide.

To order any of these books and more information about our complete range of offerings log on to

http://www.pqp.in

About Goldratt Consulting Ltd. (GC)

GC focuses on Viable Vision engagements with its clients across the globe & is headquartered out of Israel. In India, GC has been operating extensively for more than 6 years with several reputed companies in delivering highly successful Viable Vision engagements. Typical clientele industries are fast moving consumer goods, textile products, steel & commodity products, engineered goods, pharmaceutical products, retailing & Construction companies. Due to its hands on experience with Indian business & economic environment over several projects, GC has gained extensive experience in understanding the local needs & challenges, as a result well poised to deliver quick & successful implementation results in the Indian industry.

For enquiries please contact

IndiaMarketing@goldrattgroup.com (or)
visit www.goldrattconsulting.com

Obvious? Isn't It Obvious? Isn't It Obvious? Isn't It Obvious? Is

Obvious? Isn't It Obvious? Isn't It Obvious? Isn't It Obvious? Is
Obvious? Isn't It Obvious? Isn't It Obvious? Isn't It Obvious? Is
Obvious? Isn't It Obvious? Isn't It Obvious? Isn't It Obvious? Is
Obvious? Isn't It Obvious? Isn't It Obvious? Isn't It Obvious? Is
Obvious? Isn't It Obvious? Isn't It Obvious? Isn't It Obvious? Is
Obvious? Isn't It Obvious? Isn't It Obvious? Isn't It Obvious? Is
Obvious? Isn't It Obvious? Isn't It Obvious? Isn't It Obvious? Is
Obvious? Isn't It Obvious? Isn't It Obvious? Isn't It Obvious? Is
Obvious? Isn't It Obvious? Isn't It Obvious? Isn't It Obvious? Is
Obvious? Isn't It Obvious? Isn't It Obvious? Isn't It Obvious? Is
Obvious? Isn't It Obvious? Isn't It Obvious? Isn't It Obvious? Is
Obvious? Isn't It Obvious? Isn't It Obvious? Isn't It Obvious? Is
Obvious? Isn't It Obvious? Isn't It Obvious? Isn't It Obvious? Is
Obvious? Isn't It Obvious? Isn't It Obvious? Isn't It Obvious? Is
Obvious? Isn't It Obvious? Isn't It Obvious? Isn't It Obvious? Is
Obvious? Isn't It Obvious? Isn't It Obvious? Isn't It Obvious? Is
Obvious? Isn't It Obvious? Isn't It Obvious? Isn't It Obvious? Is
Obvious? Isn't It Obvious? Isn't It Obvious? Isn't It Obvious? Is
Obvious? Isn't It Obvious? Isn't It Obvious? Isn't It Obvious? Is
Obvious? Isn't It Obvious? Isn't It Obvious? Isn't It Obvious? Is
Obvious? Isn't It Obvious? Isn't It Obvious? Isn't It Obvious? Is
Obvious? Isn't It Obvious? Isn't It Obvious? Isn't It Obvious? Is
Obvious? Isn't It Obvious? Isn't It Obvious? Isn't It Obvious? Is
Obvious? Isn't It Obvious? Isn't It Obvious? Isn't It Obvious? Is
Obvious? Isn't It Obvious? Isn't It Obvious? Isn't It Obvious? Is
Obvious? Isn't It Obvious? Isn't It Obvious? Isn't It Obvious? Is
Obvious? Isn't It Obvious? Isn't It Obvious? Isn't It Obvious? Is
Obvious? Isn't It Obvious? Isn't It Obvious? Isn't It Obvious? Is
Obvious? Isn't It Obvious? Isn't It Obvious? Isn't It Obvious? Is
Obvious? Isn't It Obvious? Isn't It Obvious? Isn't It Obvious? Is
Obvious? Isn't It Obvious? Isn't It Obvious? Isn't It Obvious? Is
Obvious? Isn't It Obvious? Isn't It Obvious? Isn't It Obvious? Is
Obvious? Isn't It Obvious? Isn't It Obvious? Isn't It Obvious? Is
Obvious? Isn't It Obvious? Isn't It Obvious? Isn't It Obvious? Is
Obvious? Isn't It Obvious? Isn't It Obvious? Isn't It Obvious? Is
Obvious? Isn't It Obvious? Isn't It Obvious? Isn't It Obvious? Is
Obvious? Isn't It Obvious? Isn't It Obvious? Isn't It Obvious? Is

n't It Obvious? Isn't It Obvious? Isn't It Obvious? Isn't It Obviou
n't It Obvious? Isn't It Obvious? Isn't It Obvious? Isn't It Obviou
n't It Obvious? Isn't It Obvious? Isn't It Obvious? Isn't It Obviou
n't It Obvious? Isn't It Obvious? Isn't It Obvious? Isn't It Obviou
n't It Obvious? Isn't It Obvious? Isn't It Obvious? Isn't It Obviou
n't It Obvious? Isn't It Obvious? Isn't It Obvious? Isn't It Obviou
n't It Obvious? Isn't It Obvious? Isn't It Obvious? Isn't It Obviou
n't It Obvious? Isn't It Obvious? Isn't It Obvious? Isn't It Obviou
n't It Obvious? Isn't It Obvious? Isn't It Obvious? Isn't It Obviou
n't It Obvious? Isn't It Obvious? Isn't It Obvious? Isn't It Obviou
n't It Obvious? Isn't It Obvious? Isn't It Obvious? Isn't It Obviou
n't It Obvious? Isn't It Obvious? Isn't It Obvious? Isn't It Obviou
n't It Obvious? Isn't It Obvious? Isn't It Obvious? Isn't It Obvious
n't It Obvious? Isn't It Obvious? Isn't It Obvious? Isn't It Obvious
n't It Obvious? Isn't It Obvious? Isn't It Obvious? Isn't It Obvious
n't It Obvious? Isn't It Obvious? Isn't It Obvious? Isn't It Obvious
n't It Obvious? Isn't It Obvious? Isn't It Obvious? Isn't It Obvious
n't It Obvious? Isn't It Obvious? Isn't It Obvious? Isn't It Obvious
n't It Obvious? Isn't It Obvious? Isn't It Obvious? Isn't It Obvious
n't It Obvious? Isn't It Obvious? Isn't It Obvious? Isn't It Obvious
n't It Obvious? Isn't It Obvious? Isn't It Obvious? Isn't It Obvious
n't It Obvious? Isn't It Obvious? Isn't It Obvious? Isn't It Obvious
n't It Obvious? Isn't It Obvious? Isn't It Obvious? Isn't It Obvious
n't It Obvious? Isn't It Obvious? Isn't It Obvious? Isn't It Obvious
n't It Obvious? Isn't It Obvious? Isn't It Obvious? Isn't It Obvious
't It Obvious? Isn't It Obvious? Isn't It Obvious? Isn't It Obvious
't It Obvious? Isn't It Obvious? Isn't It Obvious? Isn't It Obvious
't It Obvious? Isn't It Obvious? Isn't It Obvious? Isn't It Obvious
't It Obvious? Isn't It Obvious? Isn't It Obvious? Isn't It Obvious
't It Obvious? Isn't It Obvious? Isn't It Obvious? Isn't It Obvious
't It Obvious? Isn't It Obvious? Isn't It Obvious? Isn't It Obvious
't It Obvious? Isn't It Obvious? Isn't It Obvious? Isn't It Obvious
't It Obvious? Isn't It Obvious? Isn't It Obvious? Isn't It Obvious
't It Obvious? Isn't It Obvious? Isn't It Obvious? Isn't It Obvious
't It Obvious? Isn't It Obvious? Isn't It Obvious? Isn't It Obvious
't It Obvious? Isn't It Obvious? Isn't It Obvious? Isn't It Obvious
't It Obvious? Isn't It Obvious? Isn't It Obvious? Isn't It Obvious
't It Obvious? Isn't It Obvious? Isn't It Obvious? Isn't It Obvious
't It Obvious? Isn't It Obvious? Isn't It Obvious? Isn't It Obvious